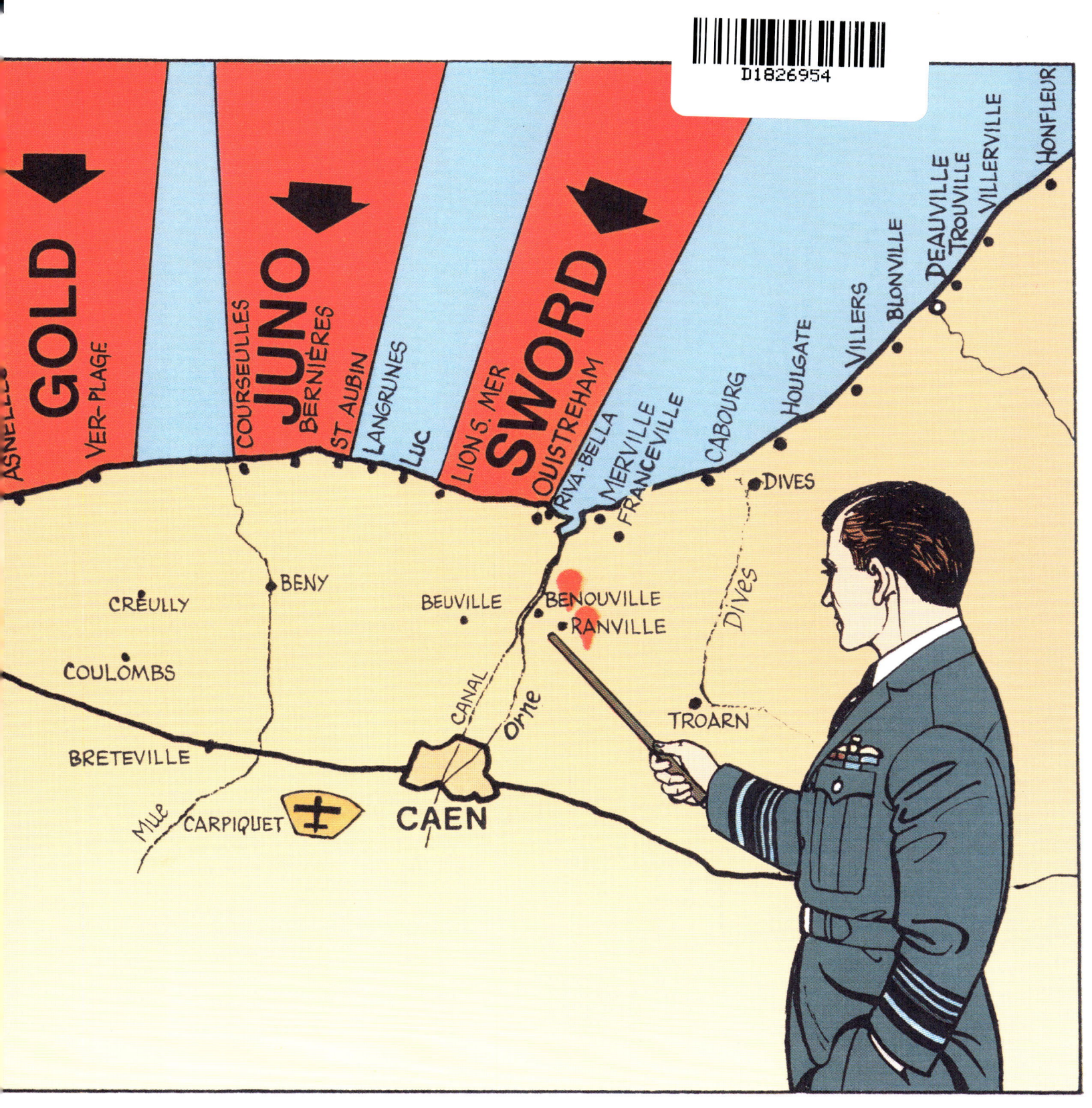

6TH JUNE 1944

OVERLORD

Script
Serge SAINT-MICHEL

Drawings
MISTER KIT

Colours
Martine BOUTIN
Laurent SAND

Historical consultants
Isabelle BOURNIER
Rémy DESQUESNES

OREP
EDITIONS

OREP Éditions, Zone tertiaire de Nonant, 14400 BAYEUX
Tel.: 02 31 51 81 31 **- Fax:** 02 31 51 81 32
E-mail : info@orepeditions.com **- Web :** www.orepeditions.com

Graphic Design: OREP
ISBN : 978-2-8151-0668-9
Legal deposit: 1st quarter 2010

APRIL, 27, 1944, NEAR PORTSMOUTH, ENGLAND, AT SOUTHQUICK HOUSE, EISENHOWER'S HEADQUARTERS...

THE 542ND SQUADRON HAS TAKEN THESE PICTURES. ONE PILOT HAS DISAPPEARED DURING THE MISSION...

IT LOOKS LIKE A GIANT UNDERGROUND CONSTRUCTION... A PLATFORM FOR DOODLEBUGS?

NO, SIR! THIS PHOTO CONFIRMS THE INFORMATION FROM THE FRENCH RESISTANCE...

4085   106W. 133. 26·APR·44. F/36"// 542 SQDN. ←

IT COULD BE A LAUNCHING PAD FOR A **GIANT ROCKET!**

GOOD LORD! THIS SCI-FI WEAPON COULD WRECK A LANDING! WE MUST BOMB IT!

SO FAR WE ARE LACKING INFORMATION ABOUT THE CONCRETE USED YET...

THE RESISTANCE WILL PROVIDE THE INFORMATION GATHERED FROM FRENCH COMPANIES WHO'VE BUILT THE SITE FOR THE GERMANS...

542 SQDN

IN THE MEAN TIME, IN FORMIGNY, NORMANDY, ON THE ROAD FROM BAYEUX TO CARENTAN...

THE 352ND GERMAN DIVISION HAS ALMOST REACHED THE COAST, HASN'T IT?

I'VE TOLD LONDON TWICE...

WIE HERRLICH LEUCHTET MIR DIE NATUR...

THEY HAVEN'T ACKNOWLEDGED RECEPTION, HAVE THEY?

NOT AT ALL!

SEND ANOTHER PIGEON, ADRIAN!

THIS ESSENTIAL PIECE OF INFORMATION COULD MAKE THE ALLIES CHANGE THEIR LANDING PLANS...

LATER...

I'VE EVEN MENTIONED THAT THE 352ND AMOUNTS TO ABOUT 12,000 TROOPS!

A LITTLE FURTHER, ON THE ROCKY COAST, IN A GERMAN OBSERVATION POST...

HANS, A PIGEON!

THESE DAYS I KILL ONE EVERY TWO OR THREE DAYS...

PANG!

FINISHED?

NO I STILL HAVE TO FIX THE CANTEEN... ROMMEL IS TO ARRIVE SOON TO INSPECT THE ATLANTIC WALL...

APRIL 26, 1944, NEAR LYME BAY, ON THE SOUTH COAST OF ENGLAND...

I HOPE IT'LL BE D-DAY SOON!

GIVE HITLER A BEATING!

PASTRYCOOKS LUNCHEON AND TEA ROOMS

CAFE

ARAGE

3

5

I HOPE THIS ONE'S FOR REAL. I'M FED UP WITH THESE PRACTICE BOARDINGS AND LANDINGS!

THE WHOLE SOUTH OF THIS COUNTRY IS A VAST ENTRENCHED ENCAMPMENT FULL OF SOLDIERS AND MATERIALS.

FINDING A GIRL AROUND HERE IS ALMOST IMPOSSIBLE SINCE ALL LEAVE HAS BEEN SUSPENDED.

WE MIGHT AS WELL FIX THE KRAUTS(1), RIGHT SERGEANT?

BUT OF COURSE, JAMES!

(1) GERMANS

SAY, SERGEANT, DO YOU REALLY BELIEVE OUR TANKS WILL FLOAT TO THE COAST WITH THESE INFLATABLE SKIRTS?

DURING ALL OUR MANOEUVRES OUR D.D.(2) PROVES SATISFACTORY...

(2) DUPLEIX-DRIVE: AMPHIBIOUS TANK

SERGEANT MIKE RILEY BELONGS TO THE 743RD TANK BATTALION (1ST AMERICAN INFANTRY DIVISION).

SO WE CAN RELY ON THEM!

PROVIDED WE DON'T LAND IN BAD WEATHER!

SERGEANT, LOTS OF MEN ARE SEASICK...

HAVE THEY TAKEN PILLS?

6

THE NEXT DAY, AT MANSTON AIRPORT (EAST COAST OF ENGLAND)...

CRASH CREW[1]! BOMBER IN DIFFICULTY APPROACHING BASE!

(1) CREW IN DANGER

WELL DAN, I'LL BET YOU TEN SHILLINGS THAT IT BREAKS IN TWO AT TOUCHDOWN!

YOU'RE DISGUSTING GORDON!

VROOAW

YOU'D DO BETTER TO SAY A PRAYER FOR THOSE POOR CHAPS!

SEVERAL SQUADRONS ARE STATIONED AT MANSTON. LOCATED ON THE COAST, IT IS ALSO A RESCUE AREA FOR PLANES IN DISTRESS WHEN RETURNING FROM A MISSION TO GERMANY.

CRAC

BANG

DAN KENWAY BELONGS TO THE 609TH SQUADRON (11TH R.A.F. FIGHTER GROUP).

REMEMBER MY BROTHER PHILIP DIED THIS WAY, FOUR DAYS AGO NEAR CHERBOURG...

I KNOW DAN, I'M SORRY!

OUR AIR-RAIDS DISORGANISE GERMAN COMMUNICATIONS AND TRANSPORT COMPLETELY...

A LITTLE LATER, IN THE SMALL MEETING ROOM OF THE BASE...

OUR BOMBINGS HAVE PUSHED THEIR OPERATIONAL AIRSTRIPS BACK FROM THE CHANNEL. WE CAN DO EVEN BETTER!

GERMAN AIRCRAFT IDENTIFICATION

THE PURPOSE OF THESE MISSIONS WAS BOTH TO WEAKEN THE ATLANTIC WALL DEFENCES AND TO DESTROY THE DOODLEBUG LAUNCHING PADS...

... AND PARTICULARLY TO FORCE THEIR SUBMARINES AND PATROL BOATS TO REMAIN BURIED IN THEIR BASES! IN SHORT, TO PREPARE OVERLORD!

FLIGHT SERGEANT MAC LAREN INTERVENES...

WHEN WILL THE FAMOUS LANDING TAKE PLACE, SIR?

GOD ONLY KNOWS, MC LAREN! DON'T BET WITH HIM!

IN THE MEANTIME, ON A BEACH IN THE SOUTH OF ENGLAND...

WHEN THE REGINA RIFLE REGIMENT LANDS IN FRANCE, THE KRAUTS WILL LOSE THEIR ARROGANCE!

FORWARD, CANADIANS!

AND HOLD YOUR RIFLES UP!

WILLIAM KEAGAN CAN HARDLY SWIM...

IF THERE ARE HOLES ON THE BEACH ON *D-DAY*, I'LL BE A GONER!

FASTER BOYS! OTHERWISE YOU'LL BE DEAD BEFORE YOU ARRIVE!

A BIT LATER...

COME ON, LIEUTENANT, TELL US WHICH PORT HAS A PEDESTRIAN PASSAGE LIKE THIS... THEN WE'LL KNOW THE LANDING PLACE!

THAT IS THE BEST KEPT SECRET ON EARTH, LE SAULT!

ON MAY 2ND, ERWIN ROMMEL INSPECTS AN ATLANTIC WALL STRONG POINT...

WHAT'S HE DOING?

TALKING SHOP!

WE MUST INCREASE THE OBSTACLES AND THE MINES ON THESE BEACHES!

EVERYTHING WILL HAPPEN HERE... IF THE ENEMY LANDS, WE'LL LOSE THE WAR!

IN FACT, THE ENEMY'S AIRFORCE WILL DESTROY OUR REINFORCEMENTS BEFORE COMING ASHORE...

I'VE SAID IT BEFORE... THE FIRST TWENTY-FOUR HOURS OF THE INVASION WILL BE DECISIVE!

BOTH FOR THE ALLIES AND FOR US, THIS WILL BE *THE LONGEST DAY!*

HERR MARSHAL, DOES OUR INTELLIGENCE SERVICE HAVE INFORMATION ABOUT THE INVASION?

NOTHING DEFINITE, BUT WE BELIEVE IT WILL HAPPEN IN THE STRAITS OF DOVER!

THE FÜHRER, ON THE OTHER HAND, IS CONVINCED IT WILL BE IN NORMANDY!

THEY'VE LEFT!

COULD WE REALLY RESIST SUCH A MASSIVE LANDING?

12ᴱ ⚡ ⚡⚡
PANZER-DIVISION "HITLERJUGEND"

IN FRANCE, IN EVREUX, AT THE HEADQUARTERS OF THE 12ᵀᴴ SS HITLERJUGEND ARMOURED DIVISION...

SURE! THAT'S WHAT THE ATLANTIC WALL IS FOR!

AND WE HAVE TEN TANK DIVISIONS BEHIND US IN FRANCE, WHICH ARE READY FOR ACTION AT THE FIRST ALERT!

OUR "USTUFS"[1] GO FOR DINNER AT SOLANGE'S, JUST LIKE EVERY WEEKEND...

I DON'T LIKE THAT PLACE! ITS CUSTOMERS LOOK LIKE TERRORISTS!

(1) UNTERSTURMFÜHRER : SUBLIEUTENANT.

G. VAN DESSEL

ON MAY 8TH, 1944, GENERAL BERNARD MONTGOMERY (COMMANDER OF THE ALLIED GROUND FORCES) RAISES AN IMPORTANT MATTER...

OUR ASSAULT TROOPS HAVE REACHED THEIR POINT OF MAXIMUM PREPARATION. WE SHOULD...

... ASSIGN THE DATE OF THE INVASION, GENERAL!

OK! CONSIDERING THE NECESSARY CONDITIONS, WHICH DATES DO THE EXPERTS PROPOSE?

THERE ARE SEVERAL POSSIBILITIES... FIRST THERE ARE MAY 21ST, 22ND, 23RD...

MUCH TOO SOON!

JUNE 5TH AND 6TH WOULD BE SUITABLE... AT THE LATEST THE 7TH THEN THE 19TH, 20TH AND 21ST OF JUNE WOULD BE ALSO GOOD!

AFTER A LONG SILENCE...

AT WHAT TIME SI LOW TIDE ON THE MORNING OF JUNE 5TH?

AT ABOUT 6.30 A.M.

AND SUNRISE?

5.50 A.M.

JUNE 5TH WILL BE THE D.DAY... IF THE WEATHER PERMITS OF COURSE!

ON MAY 15TH, 1944, THE KING OF ENGLAND HIMSELF CHAIRS A MAJOR CONFERENCE...

AIRFORCE MARSHAL A.W. TEDDER, SECOND COMMANDER-IN-CHIEF, WILL REPEAT THE SCHEDULE OF OVERLORD...

THE LANDING WILL BE MADE IN NORMANDY, BETWEEN THE ORNE ESTUARY AND THE BAY OF CARENTAN...

IT WILL TAKE PLACE ON FIVE BEACHES WITH AGREED NAMES... THE AMERICAN TROOPS WILL LAND ON UTAH AND OMAHA...

THE BRITISH AND CANADIAN TROOPS ON GOLD, JUNO AND SWORD...

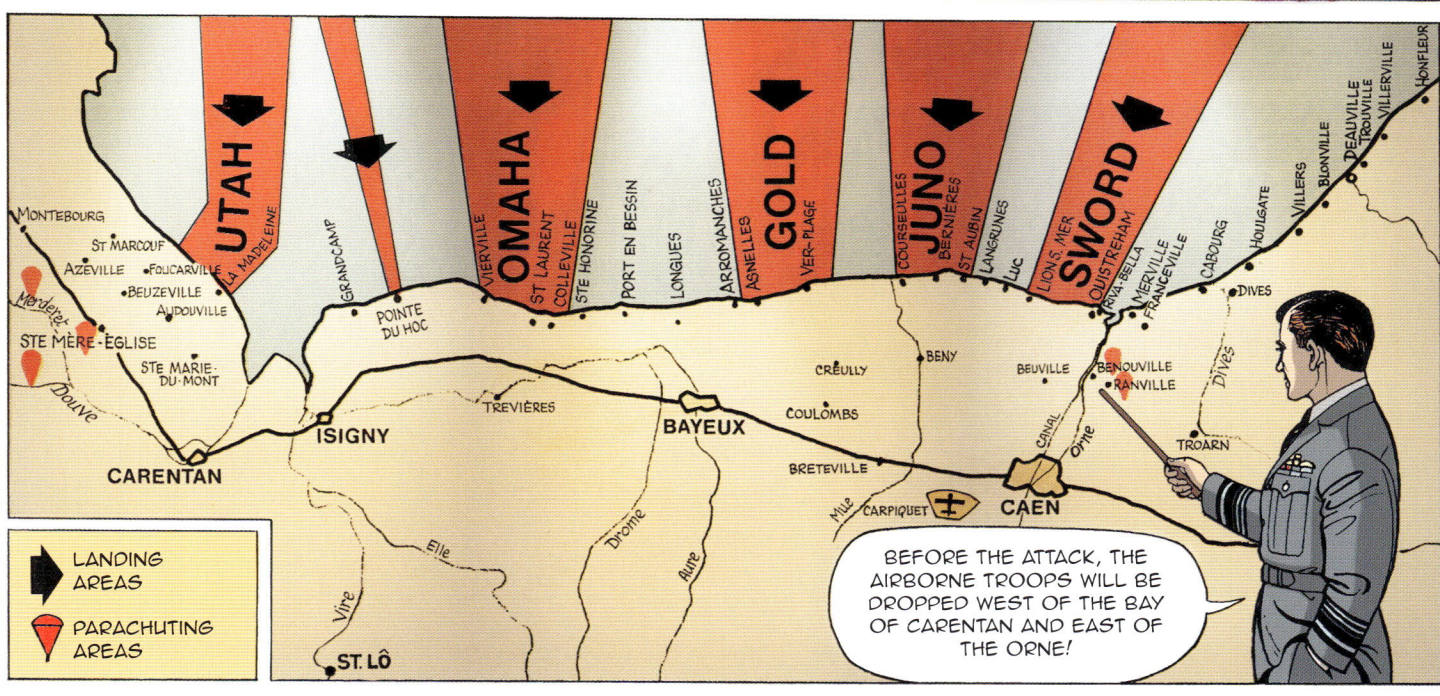

LANDING AREAS

PARACHUTING AREAS

BEFORE THE ATTACK, THE AIRBORNE TROOPS WILL BE DROPPED WEST OF THE BAY OF CARENTAN AND EAST OF THE ORNE!

AFTER INTERVENTION BY THE MILITARY STAFF, WINSTON CHURCHILL (BRITISH PRIME MINISTER) TAKES THE FLOOR...

I'VE HAD MY DOUBTS ABOUT THE SUCCESS OF OVERLORD FOR A LONG TIME, BUT NOW I FULLY SUPPORT THIS PROJECT!

A SOLEMN ROYAL SPEECH ENDS THE CONFERENCE. AND A LITTLE LATER...

I'M FURIOUS AT THE IDEA THAT THE FIRST ATTACK WILL TAKE PLACE WITHOUT ME!

IT HAS TO! ROMMEL HAS TO ASSUME THAT YOUR TANKS WILL LAND IN THE STRAITS OF DOVER!

LEAVE ME PART OF THE JOB, WILL YOU?

GENERAL PATTON, CHIEF OF THE 3RD US ARMY ● GENERAL BRADLEY, CHIEF OF THE 1ST US ARMY

LATE MAY, THE FIRST WAVE OF ASSAULT TROOPS BOARD THEIR TRANSPORT SHIPS IN HUNDREDS OF SMALL PORTS OR IMPROVISED EMBARKATION SITES.

I HOPE THIS TIME OUR PLANES AND OUR PATROLS WILL DEVASTATE THE "E-BOATS" (1)

MAY GOD HELP THEM!

THIS WRECK WILL NOT SURVIVE THE MINES!

DON'T WORRY KEAGAN! MINESWEEPERS WILL PRECEDE THE CONVOY... OF COURSE!

HEY, LE SAULT! IF WE LAND AT YOUR PLACE IN BRITTANY, INVITE US ROUND, WILL YOU?

(1) FAST GERMAN PATROL BOATS

AT THORNEY ISLAND...

SURPRISE, DAN! THE BIG CHIEF! IKE!

I KEEP TELLING ALL THE PILOTS AT THE BASES I'M VISITING... YOU'RE FANTASTIC GUYS!

BUT SOON YOU'LL BE PUSHED TO THE LIMITS OF YOUR CAPACITIES!

D-DAY'S APPROACHING!

WRAAAW

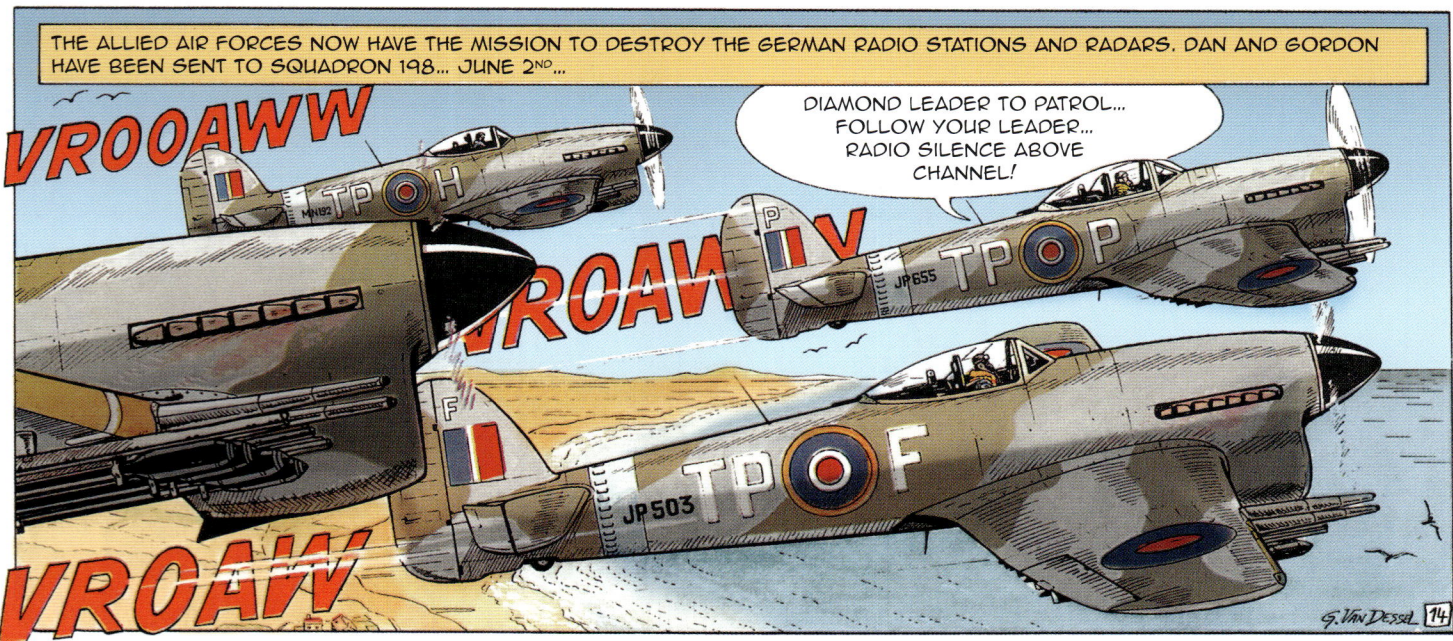

THE ALLIED AIR FORCES NOW HAVE THE MISSION TO DESTROY THE GERMAN RADIO STATIONS AND RADARS. DAN AND GORDON HAVE BEEN SENT TO SQUADRON 198... JUNE 2ND...

DIAMOND LEADER TO PATROL... FOLLOW YOUR LEADER... RADIO SILENCE ABOVE CHANNEL!

VROOAWW

VROAW

VROAW

G. VAN DESSEL 14

THEIR MISSION CONSISTS IN DESTROYING THE RADAR IN DIEPPE.

DIAMOND LEADER... TARGET IN SIGHT. *LET'S GO!*

DAN IS PENSIVE...

HERE'S HOPING I DON'T END UP LIKE MY BROTHER PHILIP!

FROM LEADER TO N°3: NEUTRALISE THE "88" AT TEN O'CLOCK BELOW... ATTACK GORDON!

O.K. DIAMANT LEADER!

BULL'S EYE!

N°3 TO LEADER... I'VE BEEN HIT...

GET AWAY FROM HERE AND HEAD BACK HOME!

A LITTLE LATER...

JUMP, GORDON! GOOD LORD, COME ON!

IMPOSSIBLE, DAN! MY BACK IS PARALYSED!

BET YOU TEN POUNDS I REACH THE BASE!

GO! JUMP! *JUMP!*

SORRY, GORDON! I SHOULD HAVE BET WITH YOU!

THE SAME DAY, IN FORMIGNY, IN NORMANDY...

DID LONDON CONFIRM THEIR RECEPTION OF OUR MESSAGE ABOUT THE 352ND?

NO! BUT GUILLAUME HAS HEARD THE FIRST LINES OF VERLAINE...[1]. IT'LL BE SOON, ADRIEN!

AND HE TOLD ME...

(1) THE LONG SOBBINGS OF AUTUMN VIOLINS...

... THAT ALL THE BRIDGES OVER THE SEINE HAVE SUFFERED REPEATED ATTACKS AND THAT ALL THE RADARS HAVE BEEN WIPED OUT...

... AT LAST, THE ALLIED AIR FORCES HAVE DESTROYED THE CORE OF GERMAN INTELLIGENCE THROUGHOUT NORTH-WESTERN FRANCE!

KOT KOT

16

IN BERLIN, THE O.K.W.(1), ON THE MORNING OF JUNE 2ND...

THE GERMAN SECRET SERVICE KNEW THAT RADIO LONDON WOULD BROADCAST THE FIRST LINE OF A POEM BY VERLAINE TO INFORM THE RESISTANCE OF THE IMMINENT INVASION.

OUR SERVICE RECEIVED THE FIRST LINE OF VERLAINE LAST NIGHT, HERR GENERAL...

GOOD! WHAT WILL THE SECOND LINE ANNOUNCE?

(1) SUPREME HEADQUARTERS OF THE GERMAN ARMY.

AN INVASION WITHIN 48 HOURS, HERR GENERAL.

I SEE THAT ALL ARMY CORPS HAVE BEEN BROUGHT TO A STATE OF EMERGENCY... PERFECT!

IN FACT, INACCURACIES IN THE TRANSMISSION OF ORDERS AND THE SCEPTICISM OF CERTAIN GENERALS PREVENTED WARNING THE ARMY IN NORMANDY... AT ROMMEL'S HQ...

THIS STORY OF THE POEM IS JUST NONSENSE! THE ALLIES WON'T LAND IN SUCH WEATHER CONDITIONS! I'M GOING TO SEIZE THE OPPORTUNITY TO LEAVE FOR GERMANY...

SUNDAY, JUNE 4TH, AT 4 A.M....

TEDDER, WE CANNOT LAND TOMORROW... D DAY WILL BE PUT OFF TILL JUNE 6TH... IF THE ANNOUNCED IMPROVEMENT IN THE WEATHER IS CONFIRMED...

GIVE THE CONVOYS THAT HAVE ALREADY SET SAIL THE ORDER TO RETURN!

O.K., IKE!

ON THE MORNING OF SUNDAY, JUNE 4TH...

SIR, ALL SHIPS HAVE RETURNED EXCEPT ONE CONVOY OF 128!

DAMN IT! THEY MIGHT JEOPARDISE OVERLORD! HAVE A FLYING BOAT. GO AND GET THEM! AND BE QUICK ABOUT IT!

A LITTLE LATER...

THERE! THE CONVOY! FLASH THE SIGNAL!

LOOK AT THAT FLYING BOAT, SERGEANT RILEY... IT'S ORDERING US TO RETURN!

WE'LL NEVER LAND... I DON'T BELIEVE IN IT ANY MORE!

MEANWHILE ROMMEL IS DRIVING TO GERMANY...

AFTER MY WIFE'S BIRTHDAY PARTY, I WILL MEET THE FÜHRER...

I'LL ASK HIM TO TRANSFER FIVE TANK DIVISIONS UNDER MY AUTHORITY AND I'LL STATION THEM ON THE COAST...

MONDAY, JUNE 5TH, BY 4 A.M., IN THE LIBRARY OF SOUTHWICK HOUSE...

SUPREME HEADQUARTERS ALLIED EXPEDITIONARY FORCES

IF THE WEATHER DOESN'T GET ANY BETTER, OVERLORD WILL HAVE TO BE POSTPONED AGAIN!

IT'S TIME TO GO! INCIDENTALLY, THE EXPERTS FORECAST A CHANGE IN THE WEATHER FOR JUNE 6TH...

WE HAVE NO CHOICE...

WE MUST ATTACK... WE WILL MAKE THE LANDINGS ON TUESDAY, JUNE 6TH!

ON THE BASE, AT THORNEY ISLAND, MONDAY, JUNE 5TH, AT NIGHTFALL...

CONTROL TO PATROL. REPEAT: YOU ARE CONFINED TO BARRACKS... IT IS FORBIDDEN TO PHONE FROM THE BASE OUTSIDE...

WE HAVE ATTACKED THE GERMAN HQ AT ST-LÔ AND BURIED ROMMEL UNDER THE BOMBS!

DAN KENWAY IS UNAWARE THAT ROMMEL HAD CANCELLED HIS VISIT TO ST-LÔ BECAUSE OF HIS JOURNEY TO GERMANY...

WHERE ARE YOU GOING WITH THIS?

PAINT BLACK AND WHITE STRIPES ON YOUR TYPHOON, SERGEANT! WE APPLY THEM TO ALL PLANES FOR OVERLORD!

WOW! SO ALL THE CONVOYS WE SAW IN THE CHANNEL ARE FOR THE INVASION! THIS TIME IT'S SERIOUS!

THE GIGANTIC INVASION IS NOW IN ACTION, THE AMERICAN PARATROOPERS TAKE OFF IN PLANES AND GLIDERS, IKE HAS A CHAT WITH THE TROOPS...

YOU'LL HAVE TO PAVE THE WAY FOR THE TROOPS WHO WILL LAND ON UTAH AND HOLD OUT TILL RELIEF COMES... I WANT TOTAL VICTORY! GOOD LUCK, BOYS!

GENERAL MAXWELL TAYLOR IS IN COMMAND OF THE 101ST AMERICAN AIRBORNE DIVISION (THE SCREAMING EAGLES)...

LET'S GO FOR IT IKE! BUT IT WON'T BE A PIECE OF CAKE!

AIRBORNE

101ST AIRBORNE

ADMIRAL BERTRAM RAMSAY (HEAD OF THE ALLIED NAVY) HAS SENT OVER 6,000 SHIPS ACROSS THE CHANNEL TO TRANSPORT OR PROJECT THE FIRST WAVE OF TROOPS...

SIR BERTRAM RAMSAY

WHAT ARE YOU THINKING ABOUT, LE SAULT?

ABOUT TWO NUMBERS... 150,000 MEN ARE GOING TO LAND IN NORMANDY AND ONLY 177 OF THEM ARE FRENCH!

AIR MARSHAL SIR TRAFFORD LEIGH-MALLORY HAS ENGAGED 12,000 PLANES AND GLIDERS IN OVERLORD. INTENSIVE BOMBINGS AND DIVERSE DISTRACTION MANOEUVRES HAVE LED THE ENEMY TO BELIEVE THAT THE INVASION WILL TAKE PLACE IN THE STRAITS OF DOVER...

COMMANDER-IN-CHIEF OF THE ALLIED AIRFORCE
SIR TRAFFORD LEIGH-MALLORY

CODED MESSAGES AND THE BBC BROADCASTING THE SECOND LINE[1] OF VERLAINE HAVE MOBILISED THE RESISTANCE IN FORMIGNY.

[1] "WOUND MY HEART WITH MONOTONOUS LANGOUR".

ADRIEN, THEY ARE BOMBING THE COAST! THEY ARE GOING TO LAND HERE, I'M SURE!

YOU KNOW WHAT YOU'VE GOT TO DO, GASTON?

YES, I DO! WITH GUILLAUME I'M GOING TO CUT THE TELEPHONE LINES SERVING CHERBOURG AND BAYEUX...

BOUM

BOUM

BOUM

BE VERY CAREFUL GASTON... THE GERMAN POLICE HAVE SUCCEEDED IN INFILTRATING OUR NETWORK...

...AND YOU CAN'T TRUST ANYONE AROUND HERE...

I KNOW! I MUST BE GOING... WITH MY FIREMAN'S PASS THE GERMANS WON'T BOTHER ME!

20

TAKING THESE TWO BRIDGES WAS VITAL TO ENABLE SENDING REINFORCEMENTS BY ROAD TO THE 6TH DIVISION THAT WAS TO BE DROPPED BETWEEN THE ORNE AND THE DIVES.

TEN MINUTES LATER, AT 0.30 A.M., ON TUESDAY, JUNE 6TH, 1944...

...IN THE CAFÉ AT THE BRIDGE OVER THE CANAL...

STRANGE! THE GERMANS SHOUTED "PARAS", THEY FIRED AND THEN NOTHING AT ALL!

THEY KILLED THEM... THE POOR CHAPS!

SOLDIERS ARE COMING NEAR...THEY ALL HAVE BLACK FACES!

WHAT DOES THAT MEAN?

ANY GERMANS IN THE HOUSE?

NO! YOU CAN CHECK... COME IN!

LATER...

MADAM, WE'VE COME TO LIBERATE FRANCE... GO TO THE BASEMENT. HEAVY FIGHTING WILL BEGIN SOON!

IN THE SOUTH OF ENGLAND, AT THORNEY ISLAND, FROM WHERE SERGEANT KENWAY'S SQUADRON OPERATES; AT 2 A.M. ...

WELL GENTLEMEN... THIS IS THE DAY... YOUR MISSION: ESTABLISH A SMOKE CURTAIN BETWEEN THE INVASION FLEET AND THE COAST OF NORMANDY...

DO NOT APPROACH THE SHIPS! THEY HAVE BEEN ORDERED TO SHOOT DOWN ANY PLANES!

THE FIGHTERS WILL HAVE THE TASK OF ENSURING FIRE-COVER AT SWORD...

AT 3 A.M. AT ABOUT TEN KILOMETRES NORTHEAST OF THE BRIDGES CAPTURED BY MAJOR HOWARD...

WE WERE DROPPED TOO FAR FROM THE TARGET, COLONEL, AND WE HAVE ONLY MANAGED TO ASSEMBLE 150 MEN OUT OF 700...

AND WE HAVE NEITHER OUR GUNS, VEHICLES, NOR OUR MINE DETECTORS, NOR...

THE 9TH BRIGADE OF THE 6TH BRITISH AIRBORNE DIVISION HAD TO CAPTURE THE BATTERY AT MERVILLE, WHOSE GUNS WERE CAPABLE OF COVERING THE ENTIRE SWORD LANDING ZONE...

LIEUTENANT-COLONEL OTWAY IS IN COMMAND OF THE NINTH BRIGADE.

NO TEARS! WE ARE GOING TO TAKE THIS BATTERY... IT'S THIS WAY!

IN THE MEANTIME 72 GLIDERS FROM THE 6TH BRITISH AIRBORNE DIVISION TOUCH DOWN NEAR RANVILLE. IT'S 3.30 A.M. ...

23

25

GENERAL GALE IS IN COMMAND OF THE 6TH DIVISION, ENTRUSTED WITH THE MISSION OF "HOLDING" THE EAST SIDE OF THE INVASION.

GENERAL RICHARD GALE

HOW ARE THE MEN?

MANY WOUNDED IN CERTAIN BRIGADES, GENERAL, AND THE WIND HAS DRIFTED THE GLIDERS WELL OFF-COURSE...

THE SIXTH WILL ALSO HAVE TO CONQUER THE HEIGHTS NORTHEAST OF CAEN AND DESTROY THE BRIDGES OVER THE DIVES (TO BLOCK GERMAN REINFORCEMENTS).

...BUT WE HAVE NEARLY ALL THE MATERIAL, GENERAL: THE ANTI-TANK GUNS, THE JEEPS, THE BULLDOZERS...

WE'LL SEND A BATTALION TO REINFORCE MAJOR HOWARD'S POSITIONS AND ANOTHER ONE TO PROTECT RANVILLE.

MEANWHILE, NEAR COTENTIN, THE TWO U.S. AIRBORNE DIVISIONS ARE PARACHUTED WITH VERY LITTLE PRECISION... AND...

TAC TAC TAC TAC TAC

FIRE!

THE PARAS PROCEED AT RANDOM, ANXIOUS AND WEARY...

LISTEN TO THOSE FOOTSTEPS... I'LL USE THE GRASSHOPPER THEY GAVE US...

IF IT'S OUR MEN, THEY'LL USE THIS DEVICE AND ANSWER WITH A CLICK-CLACK!

STOP!

NO, BILLY! IF THEY'RE KRAUTS, THIS GADGET WILL GIVE US AWAY!

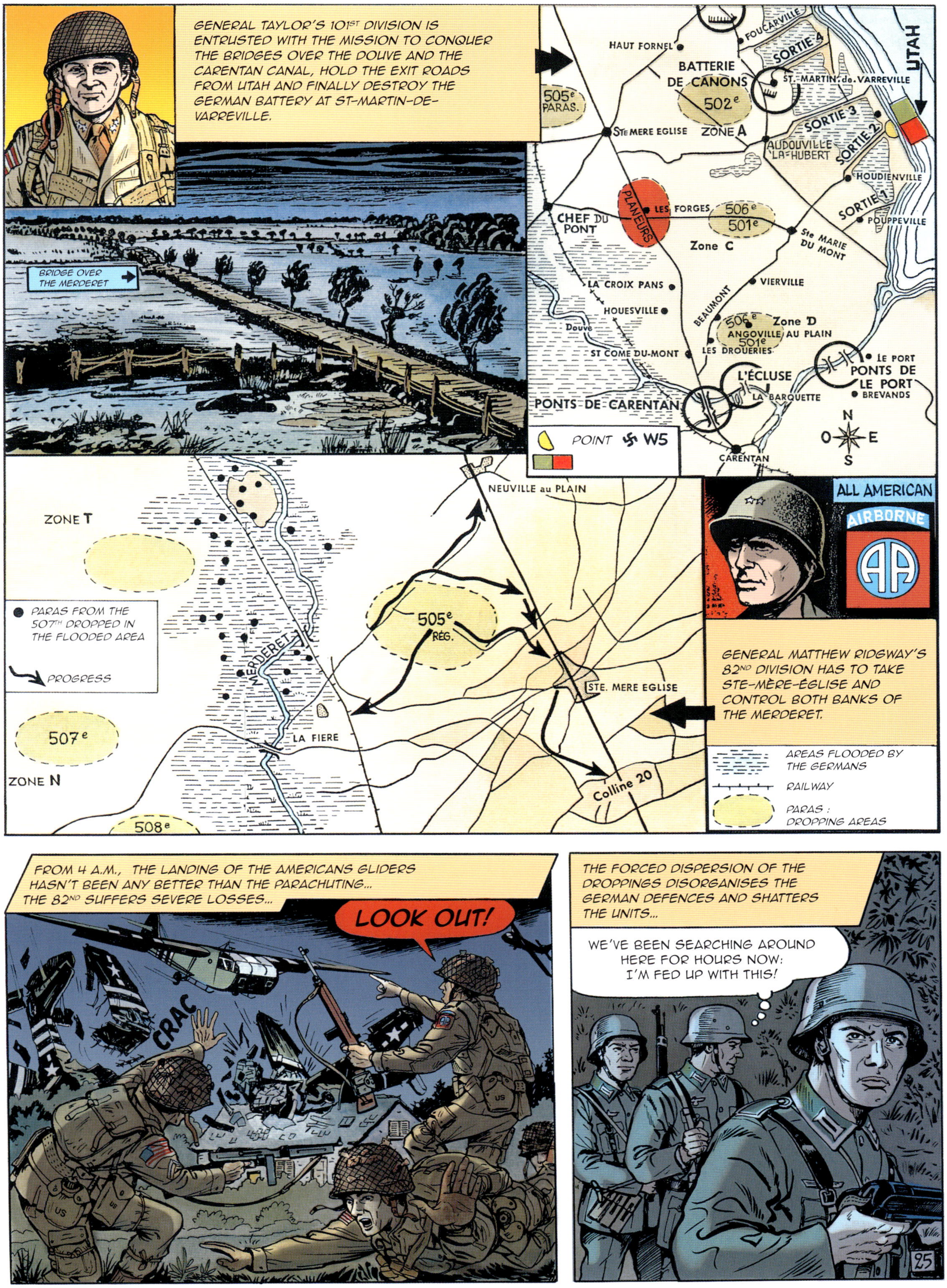

GENERAL TAYLOR'S 101ST DIVISION IS ENTRUSTED WITH THE MISSION TO CONQUER THE BRIDGES OVER THE DOUVE AND THE CARENTAN CANAL, HOLD THE EXIT ROADS FROM UTAH AND FINALLY DESTROY THE GERMAN BATTERY AT ST-MARTIN-DE-VARREVILLE.

BRIDGE OVER THE MERDERET →

Map (top right):

HAUT FORNEL · FOUCARVILLE · UTAH
SORTIE 4
BATTERIE DE CANONS 502e · ST. MARTIN de VARREVILLE
505e PARAS.
Ste MERE EGLISE · ZONE A · SORTIE 3
AUDOUVILLE LA-HUBERT · SORTIE 2
HOUDIENVILLE
PLANEURS · LES FORGES · 506e 501e
CHEF DU PONT · Zone C · SORTIE 1 · POUPPEVILLE
Ste MARIE DU MONT
LA CROIX PANS · VIERVILLE
HOUESVILLE · BEAUMONT
Douve · 505e 501e Zone D
ANGOVILLE AU PLAIN
ST COME DU-MONT · LES DROUERIES
L'ÉCLUSE · LE PORT · PONTS DE LE PORT
LA BARQUETTE · BREVANDS
PONTS DE CARENTAN
N O E S
POINT ⚛ W5
CARENTAN

Map (middle left):

ZONE T
NEUVILLE au PLAIN
• PARAS FROM THE 507TH DROPPED IN THE FLOODED AREA
↳ PROGRESS
505e RÉG.
MERDERET
Ste. MERE EGLISE
507e
LA FIERE
ZONE N
Colline 20
508e

ALL AMERICAN
AIRBORNE
AA

GENERAL MATTHEW RIDGWAY'S 82ND DIVISION HAS TO TAKE STE-MÈRE-ÉGLISE AND CONTROL BOTH BANKS OF THE MERDERET.

AREAS FLOODED BY THE GERMANS
RAILWAY
PARAS : DROPPING AREAS

FROM 4 A.M., THE LANDING OF THE AMERICANS GLIDERS HASN'T BEEN ANY BETTER THAN THE PARACHUTING... THE 82ND SUFFERS SEVERE LOSSES...

THE FORCED DISPERSION OF THE DROPPINGS DISORGANISES THE GERMAN DEFENCES AND SHATTERS THE UNITS...

EXCLUDING THE COMMANDOS DROPPED IN BRITTANY 18,000 MEN HAVE LANDED IN NORMANDY. SUCH AN IMPRESSIVE AIRBORNE OPERATION DOES NOT GO UNNOTICED. THE GERMAN STAFF IS ALARMED...

NEAR PARIS, IN ST-GERMAIN-EN-LAYE, MARSHAL GERD VON RUNDSTEDT, COMMANDER-IN-CHIEF OF THE WESTERN ARMIES, HAS BEEN WOKEN...

ALL OUR INFORMATION SOURCES REPORT MAJOR PARACHUTE DROPS AT EAST OF THE ORNE AND NORTHWEST OF CARENTAN...

THIS HERALDS A MAJOR OFFENSIVE IN NORMANDY, HERR MARSHAL!

DIVERSIONARY TACTIC, BLUMENTRITT! THE REAL INVASION WILL TAKE PLACE IN THE STRAITS OF DOVER...

GUNTHER BLUMENTRITT, CHIEF-OF-STAFF OF VON RUNDSTEDT.

BUT VON RUNDSTEDT REACTS...

I'M NOT PREPARED TO TAKE THE RISK... I'LL SEND TWO SPARE TANK DIVISIONS TO THE COAST...

THE FÜRHER MUST AUTHORISE THAT, HERR MARSHAL!

WELL THEN, ASK THE O.K.W.!

VON RUNDSTED'S HQ IN ST-GERMAIN-EN-LAYE

GENERAL ALFRED JODL DIRECTS THE OPERATIONS OFFICE AT THE O.K.W.

YOUR INFORMATION IS CONFUSED AND CONTRADICTORY, BLUMENTRITT... IT'S NOT IMPORTANT ENOUGH TO WAKE THE FÜHRER... WE'LL TALK TO HIM ABOUT THAT IN THE MORNING!

GENTLEMEN, JODL REFUSES TO WAKE THE FÜRHER... SEE YOU LATER!

?!

DONNERWETTER!

CLAC

HE HE! IT'S HOT IN NORMANDY BUT THE FÜRHER'S FAST ASLEEP!

HA HA HAHA!

!

SOLDAT SCHÖRNER, MAKE US SOME COFFEE INSTEAD OF LAUGHING LIKE A CLOWN!

AROUND 4.30 A.M. LT.-COLONEL OTWAY'S MEN TAKE THE BATTERY AT MERVILLE.

TAC TAC TAC

AAAH!

TAC TA

AFTER A FIERCE BATTLE...

WE'VE DESTROYED THE GUNS OF THIS DAMNED BATTERY AND FIRED THE YELLOW ROCKET TO SIGNAL THE SUCCESS OF OUR MISSION TO THE CRUISER "ARETHUSA"...

SEND CONFIRMATION BY PIGEON!

MEANWHILE THE 101ST DIVISION TOOK NEARLY ALL UTAH EXIT ROADS, AND THE PARAS FROM THE 82ND FREED STE-MÈRE-ÉGLISE...

AT 5 A.M. THE GREATEST ARMADA OF ALL TIMES COMES WITHIN SIGHT OF THE FRENCH COAST...

MESSAGE FROM GENERAL GALE: THE 6TH DIVISION HAS SUFFERED LOSSES BUT HAS ACHIEVED ITS GOAL.

IN CHERBOURG, AT THE KRIEGSMARINE(1) LISTENING POST...

OUR SOUND DETECTORS SIGNAL SHIP NOISES IN THE BAY OF SEINE, ADMIRAL!

TRY TO WARN THE CHIEFS OF STAFF ONCE MORE!

IT'S EXTREMELY DIFFICULT! WE'VE NO TELEPHONE AND THE ENEMY'S RAIDS HAVE DAMAGED OUR RADIO TRANSMITTERS...

(1) GERMAN NAVY

SUDDENLY, THREE E-BOATS COMING FROM LE HAVRE, EMERGE FROM THE ARTIFICIAL FOG AND HEAD FOR THE ARMADA...

FIRE!

ALL OUR BIG CHIEFS HAVE BEEN WRONGS... THE INVASION WILL HAPPEN IN NORMANDY!

ON BOARD SIR RAMSAY'S FLAGSHIP...

BY MIRACLE ONLY ONE SHIP HAS BEEN SUNK, SIR...

DOUBLE THE LOOK-OUTS AND GET THE BIG GUNS READY...

AFTER THE AIRFORCE, THE ALLIED NAVY BOMBS THE GERMANS COASTAL DEFENCES...

BAOUM BAOUM

BAOUM

DURING THE NIGHT, GENERAL TAYLOR SUCCEEDS IN REGROUPING SOME HUNDRED PARAS AND AT ABOUT 5.30 A.M. ...

BAOUM BAOUM

LISTEN TO THE ROAR OF THE GUNS... WE MUST HELP OUR BOYS TO LAND... UTAH BEACH IS OVER THERE... LET'S GO!

ONE HOUR LATER, THE FIRST PARTIES OF THE 4TH AMERICAN DIVISION (7TH ARMY CORPS) MAKE A LANDING...

"IVY"

4TH US DIV.

WE'RE NOT AT UTAH, BUT TWO KM TO THE SOUTH!

WHAT ARE THE ORDERS, GENERAL?

GENERAL TH. ROOSEVELT

WE START THE WAR HERE! WE'RE GOING TO ATTACK THE GERMAN BUNKERS FROM BEHIND! FORWARD MARCH!

IN DREUX, AT THE GERMAN AIR BASE OF THE JG3(1) FIGHTER GROUPS III AND IV...

JG 3 BADGE

RADIO BERLIN BROADCASTING ON SHORT WAVE... THE ALLIED INVASION HAS STARTED BY SEA AND BY AIR IN NORMANDY...

SIE KOMMEN!(2) AND NEARLY ALL OUR PLANES HAVE BEEN WITHDRAWN!

IT'S INCREDIBLE! WE DIDN'T EXPECT THEM THERE!

(1) JAGDGESCHWADER 3 (FIGHTER SQUADRON 3).

(2) THEY ARE COMING!

28

30

AT 6.35 A.M., THE FIRST AMERICAN DIVISION (5TH ARMY CORPS) LANDS ON OMAHA (FROM VERVILLE TO COLLEVILLE S/MER).

SILENT SO FAR, THE GERMAN DEFENCES SUDDENLY SEND A LINE OF FIRE TO THE WAVE OF ATTACKING SOLDIERS...

THE NIGHTMARE OF OMAHA BEGINS...

TAC TAC TAC TAC TAC BAOUM TAC TAC

WOUMM

TAC TAC TAC TAC
TAC TAC TAC TA

1

1ST US DIV. "BIG RED ONE"

SGT. RILEY'S SHERMAN AMPHIBIAN IS COMING ASHORE...

TAC TAC TAC TAC
TAC TAC TAC TAC

TAC TAC TAC TAC TAC
TAC TAC TAC

BAOUM

THANK PROVIDENCE, BOYS, WE HAVEN'T SUNK...

OVER HILLOCK!

THERE! ON THE KRAUTS!

FIRE! FIRE!

TAC TAC TAC TAC
BOUM

WHO'S THAT UNARMED TOURIST OVER THERE?

IT'S ERNEST HEMINGWAY, THE COLLIER'S[1] WAR CORRESPONDENT...

TAC TAC TAC-TAC-TAC-TAC
TAC

(1) US MAGAZINE, DISAPPEARED IN 1957.

...WHO'S MULLING OVER HIS ARTICLE...

DEAR READERS...HERE WE ARE EXPERIENCING A TRAGEDY... OUR BOYS ARE STUCK ON AN ILL-FATED BEACH. OUR LOSSES ARE VERY HIGH...

AT THAT MOMENT THE ENEMY'S FIRE FOCUSES ON A FEW D.D.'S STILL AFLOAT...

SERGEANT! WE'RE STUCK! WE'LL BE SCORCHED TO DEATH!

GET OUT OF HERE!

WHICH WAY?

29

SUDDENLY AN "88" FIRES...

BANG!

WE'RE LUCKY! A SHELL HAS CLEARED THE WAY!

DON'T STAY THERE! FORWARD!

SHORTLY AFTER 7 A.M. THE 2ND RANGER BATTALION ATTACKS LA POINTE DU HOC, FROM WHERE A POWERFUL BATTERY THREATENS OMAHA...

2ND RANGER BN

BAOUM

IN SPITE OF SEVERE LOSSES, A HANDFUL OF RANGERS REACH THE TOP OF THE CLIFF...

BANG

TAC TAC TAC TAC TAC TAC TAC TAC

THE BATTERY'S OVER THERE!

TAC TAC TAC TAC TAC

MEANWHILE, IN LILLE, WING COMMANDER JOSEPH PRILLER ANSWERS THE PHONE...

THEY HAVE LANDED? ... AND YOU WANT ME TO HURRY?

IS THAT A JOKE? YOU'VE ONLY LEFT ME TWO PLANES!!!

OBEY THE ORDERS PRILLER!

30

MEANWHILE THE BRITISH TROOPS HAVE SET FOOT ASHORE ON GOLD BEACH (ASNELLES AND VER-SUR-MER) AND ON SWORD BEACH (COLLEVILLE AND HERMANVILLE).

FROM LEADER... NO ENEMY FIGHTERS IN SWORD AREA... WE'RE MOVING...

WE'LL COME BACK, DAN. PROMISE!

A LITTLE LATER, KOMMODORE(1) PRILLER AND HIS TEAM-MATE HANS WODARCZYK DIVE ON SWORD...

TAC TAC TAC

TAC TAC TAC

(1) SQUADRON LEADER.

COMMANDO 4 HAS TO CLEAR THE AREA'S BASES.

TAC TAC TAC TAC TAC TAC

LOOK OUT!

TAC TAC TAC

IT ALSO HAS TO START TO REINFORCE THE 6TH AIRBORNE DIVISION EAST OF THE ORNE...

THE PRISONERS! THEY'RE ESCAPING! FIRE! SLAUGHTER THEM!

TAC TAC TAC

TAC TAC TAC TAC

AARGH!

31

A LITTLE BEFORE 8 A.M., THE CANADIANS LAND AT JUNO (FROM GRAYE-SUR-MER TO ST.-AUBIN).

BOM

BAM

GOOD LORD! ANOTHER WARCRAFT BLOWN UP... THE HIGH TIDE IS PREVENTING THEM FROM SEEING THE MINES...

AND THE SWELL IS CAPSIZING THE LANDING BARGES!

HOLD ON TO ME, WILLIE!

HELP!

BOUM

FEUER!

THE GERMAN RESISTANCE IS STRONG (CERTAIN STRONG POINTS ONLY FALLING ON JUNE 8TH). THE CANADIANS SUFFER SUBSTANTIAL LOSSES...

LONG LIVE THE REGINA'S RIFLES!

MEANWHILE, THE FRENCH MARINES ARE PROCEEDING UNDER HEAVY FIRE IN OUISTREHAM AND ARE ATTACKING THE CASINO...

TAC TAC TAC

TAC TAC TAC

1ST BATTALION F.M. COMMANDO

TAC TAC TAC

BOUM

BOM

SHOTS ARE ALSO COMING FROM THE CASINO'S BASEMENT...

COMMANDED BY PHILIPPE KIEFFER, THE FRENCH MARINES TAKE THE BUILDING BY STORM...

BAM

AT 9.33 A.M. GENERAL EISENHOWER HAS THE WHOLE WORLD INFORMED ABOUT THE LANDINGS AT LA ROCHE GUYON (NEAR PARIS) AT ROMMEL'S HQ...

HERR GENERAL, I'VE A COMPLETE REPORT ON THE INVASION... THE OFFENSIVE APPEARS TO BE VERY SUBSTANTIAL!

GENERAL HANS SPEIDEL IS MARSHAL ROMMEL'S CHIEF-OF-STAFF...

INDEED; IT'S A MASSIVE OPERATION! I WILL PHONE THE MARSHAL!

...THE INVADER IS ONLY SMALL FRY THAT WE WILL THROW BACK IN THE SEA! GET READY, GENTLEMEN!

IN EVREUX, KURT MEYER (A "HITLERJUGEND" CHIEF) HAS ASSEMBLED HIS OFFICERS...

GENTLEMEN, "THEY" HAVE LANDED, BUT WE HAVEN'T RECEIVED THE ORDER TO ATTACK YET...

BY THE END OF THE MORNING, IN FORMIGNY (5 KM FROM THE OMAHA LANDING ZONE), ON THE ROOF OF ADRIEN'S FARM...

SCRUTINISE THE LANDSCAPE GASTON, WHAT CAN YOU SEE?

NOTHING! THEY MUST STILL BE ON THE BEACH...

BLAM

NO! A TANK IS COMING ON THE COASTAL ROAD... IT'S FIRING!

ON BOARD A DESTROYER...

THANKS TO THIS SHOOTING I CAN LOCATE THE BATTERY THAT IS SLAUGHTERING OUR BOYS! COME A BIT CLOSER TO THE BEACH!

33

WE'RE TAKING RISKS, COMMANDER!

IT'S OUR SOLDIERS WHO ARE TAKING RISKS! **BLOW UP THAT BATTERY!**

SUPPORTED BY A CRUISER, THE DESTROYER CRUSHES THE MOULINS BATTERY WITH MORTAR-SHELLS!

THE KRAUTS ARE SURRENDERING! THE ROAD IS FINALLY OPEN! FORWARD!

ERNEST HEMINGWAY IS PONDERING OVER THE ARTICLE HE WILL WRITE FOR "COLLIER'S"

IN SMALL GROUPS OUR WEARY SOLDIERS ARE LEAVING THE BEACH.

IN FRONT OF US THERE IS A GREEN LANDSCAPE... I SEE BEAUTIFUL MEADOWS, A SHELLED VILLAGE, BUT NO ENEMY! AND YET, THE DEAD LAY SCATTERED ON THE BEACH...

IT'S AS IF I'D DREAMT THE BLOODY OMAHA NIGHTMARE!

AT NOON, BEFORE THE BRITISH HOUSE OF COMMONS, CHURCHILL CONFIRMS THE ALLIED CAPTURE OF ROME AND THEN DESCRIBES THE INVASION IN STYLE...

BY SEA AND BY AIR, THOUSANDS OF LINES ARE DRAWING THE LIBERATED WORLD...

AT ST.-GERMAIN-EN-LAYE...

JODL STILL REFUSES TO GIVE US THE "PANZER LEHR" AND THE 12TH SS TANK DIVISION... CALL THE FÜHRER, HERR MARSHAL! HE WON'T SAY NO TO YOU!

NO, I WON'T BEG THE FÜHRER, BLUMENTRITT...

AT 1.30 P.M. AT THE BÉNOUVILLE BRIDGE WHERE MAJOR HOWARD HAS PUSHED BACK SEVERAL GERMAN COUNTERATTACKS...

BOUM

BOUM

I'M FED UP WITH BEING UNDER FIRE WITHOUT REACTING... AND COMMANDO 4 HASN'T ARRIVED YET!

34

♪ ♪ ♪

LISTEN! I CAN HEAR "BLUE BONNET OVER THE BORDER"...

AT LAST! LORD LOVAT'S BATTALION!

♪ ♪ ♪

SORRY FOR THE DELAY, MAJOR HOWARD... WE LANDED LATER THAN PLANNED!

LE SAULT SETTLES NEAR AN ENGLISH SOLDIER...

WHAT'S UP? YOU'RE SO STRANGE... SCARED?

NO! I'VE KILLED SIX GERMAN PRISONERS... IN COLD BLOOD!

WELL, THE WAR IS ON!

I DIDN'T IMAGINE IT LIKE THIS!

MEANWHILE GENERAL TAYLOR HAS BEEN FIGHTING IN POUPPEVILLE (NEAR UTAH) FOR SEVERAL HOURS...

WE'RE TAKING THE VILLAGE AT LAST, GENERAL!

HEY! THE GERMANS ARE FLEEING!

CATCH THEM! HURRY!!

THERE THEY ARE!

35

A LITTLE LATER...

ROGER!

FROM BLUE 1 TO BLUE 2...
ARMOURED CONVOY AT TWO O'CLOCK...
LEAD THE WAY, KENWAY! *GO!*

PASS AUF! TIEFFLIEGER!(1)

(1) ATTENTION! NOSE DIVE ATTACK

TAC TAC TAC

TEUFEL! WHERE ARE OUR PLANES?

IN THE MEANTIME, ANOTHER TANK DIVISION, THE 21ST PANZER, HAS BEEN ORDERED TO ATTACK IN THE DIRECTION OF SWORD. ITS TANKS ARE MAKING THEIR WAY THROUGH CAEN...

IN THE HALLWAY, THE CAEN MEMORIAL DISPLAYS A FINE LIFE-SIZE REPLICA OF A ROCKET TYPHOON". THIS MACHINE WAS HIT BY THE FLAK ON JUNE 7TH, 1944, WHEN IT ATTACKED A RAILWAY CONVOY IN MÉZIDON STATION (CAEN-PARIS RAILWAY LINE). THE PILOT, FLIGHT SGT. J.J. ROWLAND, WAS KILLED.

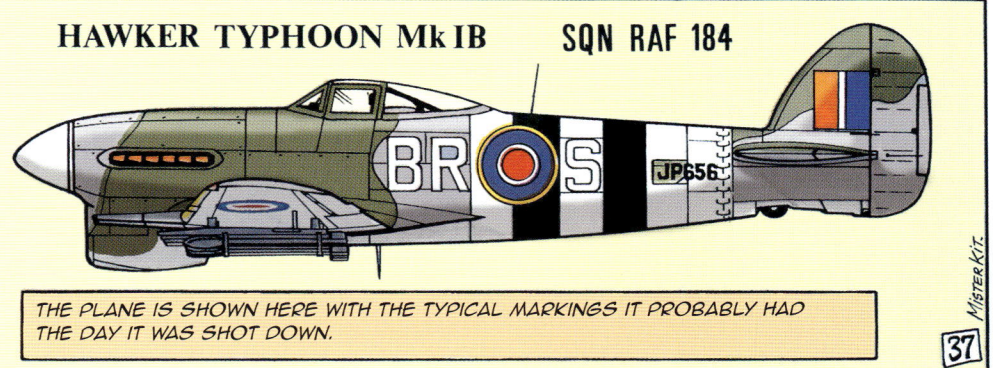

HAWKER TYPHOON Mk IB   SQN RAF 184

BROS   JP656

THE PLANE IS SHOWN HERE WITH THE TYPICAL MARKINGS IT PROBABLY HAD THE DAY IT WAS SHOT DOWN.

37

ONE UNIT SUCCEEDS IN PENETRATING AUDACIOUSLY AS FAR AS LUC-SUR-MER...

MEIN GOTT! IT'S INCREDIBLE!

THEY REALLY HAVE LANDED!

ATTENTION! ENEMY TANKS ON YOUR EAST FLANK!

GET BACK! HIDE IN THE UNDERGROWTH!

FEUER!

LATER, AT SUNSET...

THEY'RE DROPPING GLIDERS BEHIND US! GENERAL WITHDRAWAL TO CAEN!

THE GERMAN'S ARE UNAWARE THAT THE LATEST REINFORCEMENTS ARE INTENDED FOR GENERAL GALE'S 6TH DIVISION...

HEY, DON'T LEAVE OR WE'RE DONE FOR! MY DIVISION HAS SUFFERED SEVERE LOSSES!

WE CAN'T DO ANYTHING FOR YOU, HERR GENERAL!

WE'RE GOING TO BE SURROUNDED AND WE DON'T HAVE ANY SUPPORT!

YOU COWARDS! THAT'S HOW YOU LOSE A WAR!

AT LA ROCHE-SUR-YON, WHERE MARSHAL ROMMEL HAS RETURNED AT THE END OF THE DAY...

I SHOULD HAVE KNOWN THEY'D LAND IN NORMANDY!

THE 21ST PANZER'S COUNTER-ATTACK HAS FAILED, HERR MARSHAL... WILL BE ABLE TO PUSH BACK THE ENEMY?

I HOPE SO! I'VE ALWAYS WON MY BATTLES... BUT FOR NOW I'M EXHAUSTED! IT'S BEEN A VERY, VERY LONG DAY, SPEIDEL!

38

AT NIGHT, THE WAR CORRESPONDENTS TAKE THE OPPORTUNITY TO FINISH THEIR COVERAGE...

THAT MADMAN WITH THE TYPEWRITER WILL GIVE US AWAY!

HE JUMPED WITH IT, WHY SHOULDN'T HE USE IT NOW?

... I AM WITH THE 82ND AIRBORNE DIVISION SOMEWHERE IN NORMANDY, IN A RUINED FARM...

OUTSIDE, THE GENERAL IS ENCOURAGING THE MEN... WE HAVE SUFFERED SEVERE LOSSES AND WE WILL HAVE TO MAKE IT THROUGH THE NIGHT, IN SPITE OF THE EXHAUSTION...

ON GERMAN SIDE, AT THE 726TH INFANTRY REGIMENTS' COMMAND POST, NEAR COLLEVILLE (1)...

THE MAN NEXT TO ME IS A HERO... HIS NAME IS HEIN SEVERLOH... HE IS 21... WITH HIS MACHINE GUN, IN THE VIERVILLE AREA(1)...

... HE CONTINUOUSLY FIRED OVER 12.000 CARTRIDGES AT THE ENEMY FROM 6.30 A.M. TILL NOON... DESPITE HIS WOUNDS, HE MANAGED TO MAKE HIS WAY HERE...

CLOSE TO COLLEVILLE...

WE'RE HOLDING ON TIGHT TO THE COAST... IF THE KRAUTS ATTACK TOMORROW, THEY'LL THROW US BACK!

NOT SURE! THEY'VE BEEN TAKEN BY SURPRISE! LET'S HOPE THE LANDING WILL SUCCEED !

(1) OMAHA BEACH ZONE.

MEANWHILE THE RANGERS AT THE POINTE DU HOC HAVE TAKEN THE BATTERY, BUT DURING THE NIGHT THE GERMANS CONTER-ATTACK...

ERGEBT EUCH!(2) YOU'RE SURROUNDED!

SHOW YOURSELF!

PANG PANG TAC TAC TAC PANG

(2) SURRENDER!

COLONEL RUDDER COMMANDS THE RANGER BATTALION...

WE'RE RUNNING OUT OF AMMUNITION... IT WON'T BE EASY TO KEEP OUR POSITION UNTIL THE REINFORCEMENTS GET HERE...

WE'LL HOLD OUT!

RANGERS

39

41

IN SAINT-LÔ, AT THE 84TH GERMAN CORPS COMMAND POST...

COMMANDER, YOU'RE SPEAKING WITH OUR CORRESPONDENT AT BAYEUX, FRAULEIN KATRIN...

HELLO?

COMMANDER, I MUST INFORM YOU THAT THE ENGLISH TANKS ARE PARADING IN THE STREETS... BAYEUX HAS FALLEN!

IS THAT A JOKE, KATRIN?

NOT AT ALL! LISTEN...

LONG LIVE THE ALLIES!

VICTORY!

HURRAY!

AND WHAT WILL BECOME OF YOU?

I'LL GET BY...

BECAUSE THE BOYS HAVE ABANDONED ME HERE...

AT THE POINTE DU HOS, WHERE COLONEL RUDDER RESISTS THE GERMAN ATTACKS WITH UNDER A HUNDRED RANGERS... HE HAS BEEN INJURED...

SEND A SIGNAL TO THE VESSELS OUT ON THE HIGH SEA...

... THEIR GUNS MUST COVER OUR POSITION OR WE'LL BE OVERRUN BY THE ENEMY...

COLONEL RUDDER AND HIS MEN WERE ONLY TO BE RELIEVED ON JUNE 8TH, AT DAYBREACK...

40

IN ARDENNE ABBEY... (5 KM. FROM CAEN), KURT MEYER'S RESIDENCE...

WHAT HAVE YOU BEEN DOING, KERNER? I'VE BEEN WAITING FOR YOU ALL NIHGT!

THE JABOS(1) ARE ATTACKING ALL CONVOYS AND WE HAD TO DRIVE AT NIGHT AFTER HAVING HIDDEN FOR HOURS UNDER THE APPLETREES!

(1) ALLIED FIGHTERS

OK! I'LL MAKE THIS ABBEY MY COMMAND POST... YOU'LL ENSURE ITS DEFENCE!

WE NEED TO BURST THROUGH THE ALLIED FRONT WITHIN A COUPLE OF HOURS. ROMMEL'S ORDERS!

MEANWHILE, THE REGINA RIFLE REGIMENT HAS FREED THE VILLAGES OF BRETTEVILLE AND NORREY (10 KM. NW OF CAEN).

BE CAREFUL! THE NEARBY SS TANKS ARE READY TO ATTACK...

THANKS FOR THE WARNING... WE'LL TAKE UP A DEFENSIVE POSITION IN THE AREA.

SEND PATROL UNITS TOWARDS CAEN!

LT. COLONEL FOSTER "MATT" MATHESON IN COMMAND OF THE "REGINA"...

IN THE AFTERNOON, A SMALL RECONNAISSANCE GROUP COMES ACROSS A "HITLERJUGEND" UNIT...

FEUER!

PANG! TAC TAC TAC TAC

WILLIAM KEAGAN AND TERRANCE FLEE LIKE HUNTED ANIMALS...

THEY'VE HIT JIMMY!

LET'S GET AWAY FROM HERE!

KOT KOOT! KOT KOOT!

LATER...

WE'RE LOST, WILLIE!

BUT WE'RE STILL ALIVE... LET'S HEAD NORTH!

41

MEANWHILE, IN ONE OF THE TOWERS OF ARDENNE ABBEY... MEYER...

THE ENEMY TANKS ARE MANOEUVRING IN FRONT OF MY OWN ARMOURED VEHICLES... IT'S TIME TO ATTACK!

TO ALL UNITS... FORWARD!

GUN TURRET AT 290º... RANGE 400M. ... ANTI TANK SHELL... FIRE!

BAM

TARGET HIT!

THE CANADIAN LOSSES ARE SEVERE AND MANY HAVE BEEN TAKEN PRISON...

WHAT ARE WE DOING WITH THE PRISONERS, HERR UNTERSTURMFÜHRER?

VROM VROM

WHATEVER YOU WISH, BOYS... BUT DON'T WASTE TIME!

TAC TAC TAC TAC TAC TAC...

AT THE FAR SIDE OF THE FIELD...

THE BASTARDS!

NO WILLIE... THAT WILL BE OF NO USE! THERE ARE TOO MANY OF THEM!

42

JUNE 7TH, AT THE END OF THE DAY, TYPHOONS ARE HUNTING GERMAN TANKS SOUTH OF CAEN. SGT. KENWAY IS FLYING WITH HIS FORMATION...

ZOUF

FROM RED LEADER... BE WARNED! THE FLAK ARE A GOOD AIM!

FROM N°3 TO RED LEADER. THE FUSELAGE HAS BEEN HIT BY "37"'S AND...

CROOOW... CROOOW...

RADIO BREAKDOWN!

I MUST LAND SOMEWHERE... I'M TOO LOW TO BAIL OUT!

VROP... VROP...

NEARBY, IN THE RANVILLE AREA...

HOLD ON TIGHT! WE'RE COMING!

DAMN!... WHERE DID THAT PLANE COME FROM?

PHEW!

GOOD LORD! THAT WAS A NARROW SHAVE!

BANG

CRAC!

43

HOW IS THE TYPHOON PILOT?

NOTHING SERIOUS, BUT HE'S IN STATE OF SHOCK! COME ON, COWS!

MOO!

MOO!

AND ON BOARD "H.M.S. FAULKNOR", OFF THE BRITISH SECTOR...

HAVE THEY HALTED THE 12TH SS DIVISION'S ATTACK AGAINST THE CANADIANS?

YES, SIR! THANKS TO OUR NAVY GUNS...

AND THE FAMOUS 21ST PANZER?

HALTED HERE BY THE BRITISH TROOPS... OUR AIRFORCE HAS INFLICTED SEVERE LOSSES ON THEM!

PERFECT! TOMORROW MORNING, YOU'LL LAND ME IN FRANCE!

WILLIE AND TERRANCE HAVE COME TO REJOIN THEIR LINES AT BRETTEVILLE...

POWERFUL SS DIVISIONS ARE PREPARING TO ATTACK THE WHOLE AREA...

WE'VE LOCATED THEM!

THEY'RE THE ONES WHO'VE BEEN EXECUTING OUR PRISONERS, WE SAW THEM...

LET'S GO TO "MATT"! WE MUST COUNTER THIS OFFENSIVE!

UP TO JUNE 11TH, FIERCE COMBAT OPPOSES THE CANADIAN REGIMENTS AND THE "HITLERJUGEND" THROUGHOUT THE NORTH-WEST OF CAEN...

JOE LAPOINTE HIT IT WITH HIS PIAT⁽¹⁾ AND GRENADES BLEW THE CATERPILLARS...

A BIT FURTHER AND THE PANTHER WOULD HAVE BLOWN "MATT'S" C.P.

(1) ROCKET LAUNCHER

44

WHEN I ENTERED BRETTEVILLE I MISSED AN SS ON A MOTORCYCLE...

HE'S THE ONE WHO ORDERED FOR OUR PRISONERS TO BE SLAUGHTERED!

DURING THIS DRAMATIC PERIOD, DOZENS OF OTHER CANADIAN PRISONERS ARE EXECUTED AND ON JUNE 11TH...

YOU'LL JOIN YOUR NEW BASE NEAR BAYEUX... THEY NEED PILOTS... AND... AVOID GLIDERS SERGEANT KENWAY!

THAT'S A PROMISE, GENERAL! THANKS!

IS... IS THE ROAD SAFE?

ALL THE BRIDGEHEAD LINKS UP TO AND INCLUDING OMAHA HAVE BEEN SECURED AND ALL THE POCKETS OF RESISTANCE HAVE BEEN OVERCOME!

THE BELGIAN COLONEL RAYMOND LALLEMANT (NICKNAMED "HORSE") WELCOMES DAN ON BEHALF OF SQUADRON 609...

WELCOME TO BASE B7 SGT KENWAY! AS SOON AS THE COMMANDOS RELOAD OUR PLANES, WE'LL BE OFF!

IS THAT WHAT THEY CALLED THE AIRFIELD? WE'LL HAVE TO MOVE THE COWS BEFORE WE TAKE OFF?

IT'S NOT AN AIRFIELD BUT A FAKE TARGET FOR THE GERMANS MORTARS!

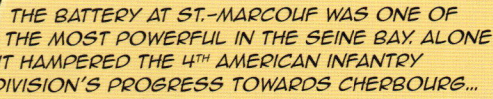

THE BATTERY AT ST.-MARCOUF WAS ONE OF THE MOST POWERFUL IN THE SEINE BAY. ALONE IT HAMPERED THE 4TH AMERICAN INFANTRY DIVISION'S PROGRESS TOWARDS CHERBOURG...

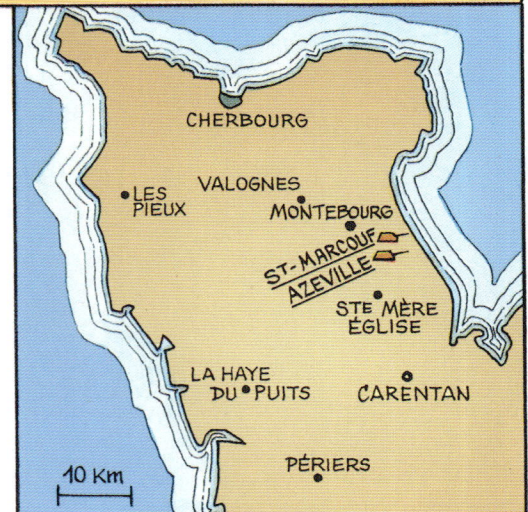

THE BASE HAS BEEN SURROUNDED SINCE JUNE 7TH...

THE KRAUTS IN THERE HAVE 600 TONS OF BOMBS AND THE DAY BEFORE YESTERDAY THEY WERE STILL SHOOTING AT UTAH...

THEY'VE EVEN BEEN SHOT BY THEIR OWN BATTERY AT AZEVILLE TO DRIVE US BACK!

THE SAME DAY, JUNE 11TH, THE CENTRAL BUNKER...

LIEUTENANT OHMSEN... I'M LISTENING!

THIS IS ADMIRAL HENNECKE AT CHERBOURG... HOW MANY MEN DO YOU HAVE LEFT, OHMSEN?

ABOUT 80, WITHOUT THE SERIOUSLY INJURED...

TRY TO GET OUT OF THERE! OUR POSITIONS ARE ONLY 10 KM. AWAY!

BURN ALL THE SECRET DOCUMENTS... TONIGHT WE'LL BE SNEAKING THROUGH THE ENEMY LINES...

THE SAME EVENING IN CARENTAN, SOUTH OF THE CITY...

HEIL HITLER! MY SS DIVISION IS ON ITS WAY TO REINFORCE YOUR PARAS... WHERE IS THE AMERICAN ADVANCE GUARD, HERR COLONEL?

YOU'RE TOO LATE! THE ENEMY HAS INFILTRATED THE ENTIRE CITY!

COLONEL BARON VON DER HEYDTE, COMMANDER OF THE 6TH REGIMENT OF FIGHTER-PARACHUTISTS.

46

THE LIBERATION OF CARENTAN ENSURES LINKS BETWEEN ALL INVASION AREAS. MONDAY JUNE 12TH...

THESE LUNATICS HAVE MANAGED TO DISAPPEAR, LEAVING BEHIND A SCORE OF UNTRANSPORTABLE WOUNDED...

THOSE "LUNATICS" AS YOU CALL THEM ARE SO COURAGEOUS!?

GENERAL, THE BATTERY AT ST.-MARCOUF HAS BEEN EVACUATED BY THE ENEMY!

YOU HAVE FINISHED THAT SATANIC BATTERY AT LAST! NOT A MINUTE TOO SOON...

GENERAL COLLINS IS IN COMMAND OF THE 7TH ARMY CORPS.

I'LL FINALLY BE ABLE TO ADVANCE TO MONTEBOURG, CUT OFF THE PENINSULA AND ATTACK CHERBOURG...

VIVE CHURCHILL!

VIVE WINNIE!

JUST AFTER NOON, IN THE JUNO LANDING ZONE...

AND LATER, IN CREULLET CASTLE, MONTGOMERY'S NEW HQ (BETWEEN COURSEULLES AND BAYEUX)...

WELL THEN. WHAT'S HAPPENING OUT IN THE FIELD?

WE'RE HAVING TROUBLE PENETRATING THE FRONT LINE NORTH OF CAEN...

WE'LL DO AN ENCIRCLING MANOEUVRE TO THE WEST AND SOUTHWEST, SIR...

... AND WE'RE IN THE STORE FOR FIERCE COMBAT WITH THE 12TH PANZER SS CLOSE TO TILLY...

FORMIGNY
PORT-EN-BESSIN
ARROMANCHES
SULLY
LA SEULLES
BAYEUX
AGY
BROUAY
NORREY-EN-BESSIN
LA DRÔME
L'AURE
BALLEROY
TILLY
JUVIGNY
CAEN →
NOYERS
L'ODON
OLIVRY
EVRECY
CAUMONT
TRACY-BOCAGE
VILLERS-BOCAGE
AUNAY-S/ODON
47

49

AND THE AMERICANS FROM THE 5TH CORPS?

THEY HAVE PASSED CAUMONT AND ARE THREATENING THE ENEMY'S WEST FLANK... I'LL BE TAKING ADVANTAGE OF THAT!

OUR "DESERT RATS" ARE MAKING A MOVE TO ENCIRCLE THE PANZER-LEHR!

BALLEROY
TILLY
BOCAGE
VILLERS BOCA

MONTY'S BERET

AMONG HIS REMARKABLE COLLECTION OF UNIFORMS THE BATTLE OF NORMANDY MEMORIAL MUSEUM IN BAYEUX DISPLAYS MARSHAL MONTGOMERY'S AUTHENTIC AND FAMOUS BLACK BERET.

INDEED 300 TANKS FROM 7TH BRITISH DIVISION (THE FAMOUS "DESERT RATS") ARE PROCEEDING TOWARD VILLERS-BOCAGE...

"THE DESERT RATS"

MEANWHILE SGT. RILEY IS WITH THE 5TH AMERICAN CORPS IN THE CAUMONT AREA...

HAVE YOU HEARD ABOUT CHEWING GUM?

TRY OUT CIDER, IT'S THE TRADITIONAL DRINK IN NORMANDY...

5

THAT'LL DO! START THE ENGINES... LET'S GO!

VROM

1

IN ST. GERMAIN-EN-LAYE, AT VON RUNDSTEDT'S H.Q....

BAD NEWS, HERR MARSHAL... THE COMMANDER OF THE 64TH ARMY CORPS GOT KILLED NEAR ST-LÔ...

GENERAL ERICH MARCKS IS DEAD?

AN ATTACK BY THE "JABOS" DID HIM IN, HERR MARSHAL!

HE WAS A GREAT SOLDIER, BLUMENTRITT, A FINE MAN AND A FRIEND...

48

AROUND 8.30 A.M. ON TUESDAY, JUNE 13TH, AT THE EASTERN EXIT OF VILLERS-BOCAGE...

YES, YES, MY EARS HAVEN'T FOOLED ME! THE "DESERT RATS" INDEED!

OBERSTURMFÜHRER[1] MICHAEL WITTMANN HAS DESTROYED 117 OF THE ENEMY'S TANKS IN RUSSIA. HIS 57 TONS "TIGER" BOUNCES...

RANGE 70 M.... ANTI-TANK SHELL! ASK FOR REINFORCEMENTS...

VROAW

(1) LIEUTENANT

WITTMANN HEADS FOR A COLUMN OF BRITISH "CROMWELLS" AND PROVOKES A DISASTER...

1ST ᛋᛋ PZ. CPS. BADGE

WHAM

BAM BAM BAM

A DOZEN "TIGERS" ARE COMING TO JOIN US, HERR OSTUF![1]

(1) ABBREVIATION FOR "OBERSTURMFÜHRER".

A STREET FIGHT LENGTHENS THE "TIGER" TANKS ATTACK, THE BRITISH ATTEMPT TO BREAK THROUGH HAS FAILED AND VILLERS-BOCAGE FALLS BACK INTO THE HANDS OF THE PANZER-LEHR...

PANZER-LEHR DIVISION

TAC·TAC·TAC

MEANWHILE...

WELL, DAN, YOU'RE OK?

NO! THE DUST, THE NOISE, NIGHT AND DAY, THE GERMAN SHELLS, I'M FED UP WITH IT!

LET'S NOT COMPLAIN TOO MUCH... FLYING BOMBS[1] ARE FALLING ON LONDON!

(3) THE V1'S

49

51

THAT NIGHT, JUST LIKE THE PREVIOUS NIGHTS, AT THE ORNE BRIDGEHEAD, NEAR AMFREVILLE...

I CAN'T GO ON! NOT A MINUTE'S REST FOR A WEEK NOW. AND ONLY DEFENSIVE COMBAT...

...AND THEY'RE LETHAL! WE SEEM TO HAVE LOST HALF OUR MEN SINCE THE LANDING...

ARE YOU SURPRISED, THERE ARE FIVE OR SIX TIMES AS MANY TROOPS ON THE OTHER SIDE... HEY! LOOK AT THAT... BUT... BUT...

BUT...

BUT HE'S ONE OF OURS!

DON'T GO LE SAULT!

WE CAN'T LEAVE HIM THERE!

PANG TAC TAC TAC

COVER ME!

PIOUWW PIOUWW PIOUWW PIOUWWW

IT'S LIEUTENANT LONGREEN! HE'S STILL ALIVE... WE MUST EVACUATE HIM! ...

TAC TAC TAC PANG PANG

THE LIEUTENANT WAS INJURED WHEN RETURNING FROM A MISSION BEHIND THE ENEMY LINES, IT WILL TAKE A DAY TO BRING HIM BACK!

TAC TAC TAC TAC

CLAC

TAC TAC TAC

SLEEVE INSIGNA WORN BY COMMANDER KIEFFER'S FRENCH COMMANDOS.

FRANCE

N° 4 COMMANDO

THE 4TH COMMANDO MUSEUM IN OUISTREHAM DISPLAYS A WIDE RANGE OF PERSONAL EFFECTS HAVING BELONGED TO THE FRENCH COMMANDOS. TOGETHER WITH AN ARRAY OF ALLIED AND GERMAN EQUIPMENT.

ON JUNE 14TH, GENERAL DE GAULLE LANDS IN THE VICINITY OF JUNO BEACH THEN TRAVELS TO BAYEUX WHERE HE IS GIVEN AN ENTHUSIASTIC WELCOME.

M5537365

VROM

50

ON JUNE 16TH, MONTGOMERY WELCOMES KING GEORGE VI AT HIS HQ IN CREULLET. ON MONDAY, JUNE 19TH, TILLY IS TAKEN.

DAMN IT! THE CITY HAS BEEN RAZED TO THE GROUND!

HARDY SURPRISING, IT TOOK OVER 30,000 SHELLS!

MINE CLEARING CONTINUES... AN ENGINEER PLACES A SIGN WARNING THAT THE SIDES OF THE ROAD ARE MINED.

MINES IN VERGES

IN ST.-GERMAIN-EN-LAYE, AT VON RUNDSTEDT'S HQ...

WE CAN BLOCK THE ENEMY SOUTH OF TILLY AND CAUMONT, BUT THE AMERICANS ARE MOVING TO CHERBOURG WITH THREE DIVISIONS...

IF WE COULD FIRE V1'S ON TO THE LANDING BEACHES, THAT WOULD HELP US A LOT!

I SUGGESTED THAT TO THE FÜHRER... BUT HE OVERRULED ME! HE WANTS TO DESTROY LONDON!

AND THE REINFORCEMENTS?

ARROMANCHES

BAYEUX

CAEN

BECAUSE OF THE JABOS AND THE RESISTANCE ATTACKS ON THE RAILWAY LINES THEY ARE ARRIVING MUCH TOO LATE.

ARROMANCHES

BAYEUX

CAEN

THE 2ND SS PANZER LEFT TOULOUSE IN THE EVENING OF JUNE 6TH... IT HASN'T ARRIVED IN NORMANDY YET!

I FEEL SORRY FOR THOSE GUYS- THEY'VE SURELY HAD THEIR LOT BY NOW!

AND WHAT ARE OUR SUBMARINES DOING?

IT SEEMS NONE HAVE SUCCEEDED IN GETTING NEAR THE TRAFFIC AREA, HERR MARSHAL...

DONNERWETTER!

ON TUESDAY, JUNE 20TH, IN SOTTEVAST (BETWEEN CHERBOURG AND VALOGNES)...

WHAT'S THAT GIANT BUILDING SITE FOR?

THE GERMANS SAID IT WAS TO LAUNCH A TERRIBLE WEAPON.

51

V2 – LAUNCHING BASE, SOTTEVAST (CHANNEL). PLAN OF THE PROJECTED SITE HAD CONSTRUCTION BEEN COMPLETED.

N

180 M

51 M.

56 M.

PARTS CONSTRUCTED AT THE END OF JUNE 1944.

A SUPER FLYING BOMB.

THEY MENTIONED A GIANT TORPEDO!

WELL, IT WAS HIGH TIME WE ARRIVED!

HOW DO WE REACT TO THE AMERICAN ULTIMATUM, HERR GENERAL?

WE DON'T FÖRSTER! WE'LL HOLD OUT AS LONG AS POSSIBLE... TILL DEATH...

THE GERMANS HAD TRANSFORMED CHERBOURG, ALREADY FORTIFIED IN THE 19TH CENTURY, INTO A STRONGHOLD CROSSED WITH TUNNELS AND SUBTERRANEAN BATTERIES. SINCE JUNE 23RD, GENERAL COLLINS' TROOPS HAVE BEEN OCCUPYING THE HEIGHTS THAT DOMINATE THE CITY...

GENERAL KARL VON SCHLIEBEN LEADS THE ULTIMATE RETALIATION FROM HIS UNDERGROUND HQ IN VILLA MAURICE IN OCTEVILLE.

OUR STRONG POINTS ARE FALLING ONE BY ONE, HERR GENERAL... THE SURVIVORS ARE ALL CRAMPED HERE IN OUR SHELTERS...

AND THE ROULE FORTRESS?

STILL HOLDING OUT... BUT FOR HOW LONG?

BAM!

I DON'T WANT TO DIE IN THIS HOLE, WILHEM!

CALM DOWN, OLD FELLOW!

52

MONDAY, JUNE 26TH...

THE ROULE FORTRESS SURRENDERED DURING THE NIGHT, HERR GENERAL... THE FORT DES FLAMANDS IS ON FIRE AND THE FOURCHES BULWARK HAS ALSO FALLEN!

THE AMERICANS ARE THROWING GRENADES DOWN OUR VENTILATION SHAFTS... OUR SHELTERS ARE HELL ON EARTH AND THE AIR THERE IS UNBREATHABLE...

MMM...

LIEUTENANT OHMSEN HAS REQUESTED TO BE RECEIVED BY ADMIRAL HENNECKE...

I PROPOSE SHOOTING ON THE ENEMY POSTED ON THE HEIGHTS... I DID THAT IN MARCOUF!

BRILLIANT IDEA! LET'S CALL THE CAP DE LA HAGUE BATTERIES.

THE AUDERVILLE BATTERIES HAVE BEEN BOMBED TO SUCH AN EXTENT THAT THEY CAN NO LONGER FIRE ACCURATELY! YOUR PLAN WON'T WORK, LIEUTENANT! A PITY!

EARLY IN THE AFTERNOON...

VON SHLIEBEN AND HENNECKE ARE SURRENDERING... WARN GENERAL EDDY AND "BLITZ JOE"(1)...

(1) GENERAL COLLINS' NICKNAME

THERE THEY ARE!

WHEREAS ON TUESDAY, JUNE 27TH, AT THE NAVY HQ, WEST OF PARIS...

WHAT? ONE OF OUR MARINE OFFICERS HAS THE KEY TO IGNITE ALL MINES ROUND CHERBOURG?

YES, ADMIRAL

HE'S MANAGED TO GET BACK TO FORT WEST(2) WITH A SAILING SHIP AND TWO WHALE SLOOPS! THE AMERICANS MUST BE FURIOUS!

(2) AT THE PORT EXIT...

THE NEWS (LARGELY EXAGGERATED BY THE O.K.W.) DRIVES "BLITZ JOE" MAD...

BAF

BOMBED FOR 3 DAYS, THE BUNKER HOUSING THE FAMOUS KEY IS FINALLY SMASHED AND, WITH IT, THE DEVICE THAT COULD WELL HAVE BLOCKED THE ENTIRE PORT.

I WANT FORT WEST SMASHED WITH MORTAR-SHELLS! GET ON WITH IT!

53

55

ON THURSDAY, JUNE 29TH, VON RUNDSTEDT AND ROMMEL DRIVE TO GERMANY ON ADOLF HITLER'S DEMAND...

POOR DOLLMANN(1)... THE FALL OF CHERBOURG PROVED TO BE A FATAL BLOW... HE DIED OF A HEART ATTACK LAST NIGHT...

A HEART ATTACK? I DIDN'T KNOW HE WAS ILL...

(1) CHIEF OF THE 7TH GERMAN ARMY (THE ARMY OF NORMANDY)

HIS CHIEF OF STAFF GAVE ME THE NEWS OVER THE PHONE THIS MORNING(2)...

(2) GENERAL DOLLMANN IN FACT COMMITTED SUICIDE.

THE NEXT DAY IN CHERBOURG...

RADIO CHERBOURG... WE CAN REPORT THAT TODAY THE LAST GERMAN RESISTANCE POSTS HAVE BEEN DESTROYED...

A CERTAIN SADNESS REIGNS OVER THE CITY DESPITE VICTORY... FOR THE ENEMY HAS APPLIED ITS STRATEGY OF SYSTEMATIC DESTRUCTION.

ONCE ONE OF THE MOST MODERN PORTS IN THE WORLD, CHERBOURG IS NOW BUT A DEVASTATED CITY! THAT WAS THE NEWS BY IMLAY WATTS...

ELSEWHERE IN CHERBOURG...

HELLO...I'D LIKE TO SEE A MILITARY CHIEF... I'VE FOUND A PLATE ON A FRAGMENT OF A PLANE...

THE AIRCRAFT CRASHED NEAR OUR FARM ON APRIL 26TH... I'VE NOTED DOWN THE DATE!

VERY GOOD, BOY... IT'S THE ID PLATE OF A BRITISH PLANE...

...WE'LL SEND IT TO THE R.A.F.!

54

WHAT'S HAPPENED WHILE I WAS WITH THE FÜHRER?

MONTGOMERY'S OFFENSIVE WAS HALTED AT THE ODON, BUT WE'LL NEVER MAKE IT BACK TO THE SEA AGAIN, HERR MARSHAL...

OUR LOSSES IN MEN AND EQUIPMENT ARE SO HIGH THAT THE UNIT CHIEFS ARE ASKING FOR THE WITHDRAWAL OF THE FRONT LINE...

SPEIDEL! I AGREE! INFORM VON RUNDSTEDT!

THE MARSHAL ALSO ACCEPTS THIS PROPOSAL AND TRANSMITS IT TO THE O.K.W. ... A LITTLE LATER...

SORRY, HERR FELD-MARSCHALL, THE FÜHRER HAS TURNED DOWN YOUR REQUEST... ANY WITHDRAWAL IS STRICTLY FORBIDDEN!

IN THAT CASE HE CAN RELIEVE ME OF MY DUTY AS COMMANDER!

THE NEXT DAY...

I'VE COME TO TELL YOU THAT THE "BOSS" HAS BEEN DISMISSED...

THEY FIRED HIM?

... FOR "HEALTH REASONS"! IT MAKES ME SICK!

HE WAS STRICT BUT FAIR!

WHO'S REPLACING HIM?

VON KLUGE! ... BUT... KEEP IT TO YOURSELF!

MARSHAL VON KLUGE

AT THE SAME TIME NEAR THE FRONT...

FELLS GOOD TO FLY!

DAN, THE "WING"(1) WANTS TO SEE YOU... HURRY!

VVRR

(1) SQUADRON LEADER

THEY FOUND THE ID PLATE AND THE DEBRIS OF YOUR BROTHER'S "SPIT" NEAR CHERBOURG. HIS DEATH IS NOW OFFICIAL SERGEANT...

NOW IT'S UP TO ME TO LOOK AFTER OUR PARENTS...

55

GENTLEMEN, WE'RE FINALLY GOING TO WAR! I PREDICT THAT YOUR NAMES WILL EITHER GO DOWN IN HISTORY OR WILL BE ON THE LISTS OF THE WAR DEAD. THANK YOU!

AFTER CAPTURING CHERBOURG, THE AMERICAN TROOPS RETURN SOUTH, BUT PROGRESS IS SLOW AND PAINSTAKING FROM CARENTAN ONWARDS...

WHAT A PLACE! HEDGES, SMALL FIELDS, HILLOCKS EVERYWHERE...

HEY! IT'S NOT TEXAS.

NO KRAUTS ANYWHERE. WE'RE NOT GOING TO HANG AROUND HERE!

piuuuww

PANG!

"THE BATTLE OF CAEN" BEGINS ON TUESDAY JULY 4ᵀᴴ, AND THE "REGINA" ATTACKS NORTHWEST OF THE CITY...

SUDDENLY...

CAREFUL! PANZERS!

LET ME GET ONE!

I'LL WAIT FOR IT TO PASS... IF ITS TANK ISN'T FULL, THE FUEL VAPOURS WILL IGNITE EASILY!

YEP! ... BUT THERE'S ANOTHER TANK...

I'LL ZERO IN ON THAT ONE!

56

WHAM!

LATER, IN BRIGADEFÜHRER KURT MEYER'S FORMER HQ...

THAT SS ESCAPED! HE WAS LUCKY!

THE TIDE MAY TURN...

NEW BOMBINGS HAVE PAVED THE WAY FOR THE FINAL ATTACK ON CAEN...

AND, ON JULY 9TH...

OUR POSITIONS HAVE BEEN DESTROYED ONE BY ONE, HERR BRIGADEFÜHRER... WHAT ARE THE ORDERS?

RETREAT... I KNOW THEY ARE NOT THE OFFICIAL INSTRUC-TIONS. BUT I PERSONALLY ORDER YOU TO RETREAT!

IN CAEN THE LOCAL POPULATION, WHICH HAS SUFFERED MUCH OVER THE PAST MONTH, IS NOW JOYFUL...

PALAIS DE JUSTICE

ALLIED SOLDIERS, V.A.D.S AND MEMBERS OF FRED SCAMARONI'S RESISTANCE FRATERNISE...

NEVERTHELESS, THE ARE TO WAIT UNTIL JULY 18TH BEFORE FIRING ON THE CITY ENDS AND, WITH IT, ANY THREAT OF GERMAN COUNTERATTACK.

58

LONG LIVE AMERICA!

LONG LIVE DE GAULLE!

THIS IS RADIO CHERBOURG... ON THIS FRIDAY, JULY 14TH, THE FRENCH NATIONAL HOLIDAY IS CELEBRATED WITH PARTICULAR ENTHUSIASM IN THE LIBERATED CITIES...

IN CHERBOURG, WITH ALLIED FLAGS FLYING EVERYWHERE, AMERICAN TROOPS AND FRENCH NAVY FIREMEN MARCH SIDE BY SIDE...

CHERBOURG INHABITANTS PROUDLY EXHIBIT THE CROSS OF LORRAINE, THE SHOULDER INSIGNIA WORN BY THE 79TH AMERICAN DIVISION[1], WHICH CAPTURED THE FORTRESS!

(1) THIS DIVISION HAD FOUGHT IN LORRAINE DURING THE GREAT WAR.

AFTER THE "HEDGEROW WAR", THE AMERICANS FIGHT FIERCELY TO THE NORTH OF SAINT-LÔ.

TAC TAC TAC TAC TAC

GERMAN PARAS!

BUT, A LITTLE FURTHER AWAY, BEHIND AN EMBANKMENT...

WOUFF

WHAM

59

61

THE FIGHTERS BELONG TO THE 602ND R.A.F. SQUADRON. THEIR LEADER "CHRIS" LEROUX LAUNCHES THE ATTACK...

FASTER, DANIEL! TRY TO REACH THE VILLAGE!

DIVE!

ACHTUNG!(1)

VRROOOAWW

(1) ATTENTION!

EACH OF THE SPITS' CANONS FIRE 10 MORTARSHELLS PER SECOND...

BAM BAM BAM
BAM
BAM
BAM
BAM

ROMMEL AND HIS DRIVER ARE HIT...

WELL DONE, CHRIS! YOU GOT THEM!

SQUADRON LEADER J.J. "CHRIS" LE ROUX (D.F.C.& 2 BARS). SOUTH AFRICAN PILOT, DISAPPEARED ON AUGUST 29TH, 1944.

LATER, IN A NEARBY HOUSE...

SORRY... YOUR MAN'S IN A BAD WAY!

THERE'S A CAR COMING... STOP IT...

A GERMAN ARMY MECHANIC, WHO JUST HAPPENED TO BE PASSING BY, TRANSPORTS THE WOUNDED MAN TO LIVAROT...

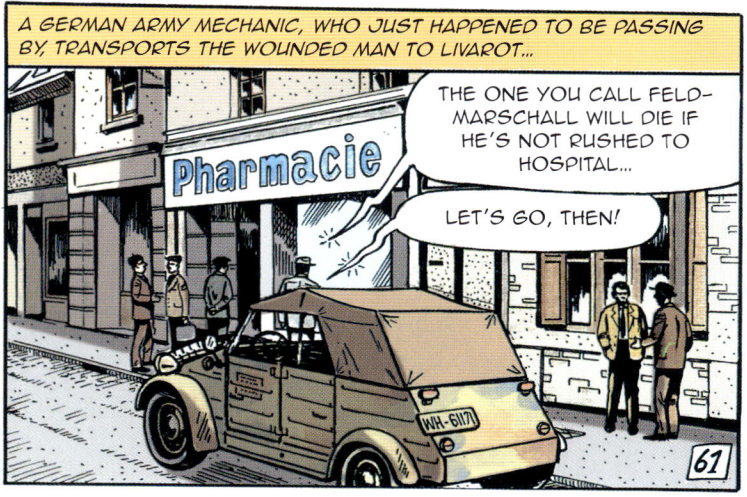

THE ONE YOU CALL FELD-MARSCHALL WILL DIE IF HE'S NOT RUSHED TO HOSPITAL...

LET'S GO, THEN!

Pharmacie

61

63

THE NEXT DAY, IN ST.-GERMAIN-EN-LAYE...

KEEP THIS TO YOURSELVES, GUYS, THE NEWS IS STILL SECRET... ROMMEL HAS BEEN SERIOUSLY INJURED BY THE BRITISH FIGHTER PLANES...

HIS DRIVER GOT KILLED... WHAT A STORY! HADN'T THEY HEARD OF OUR SECRET ANTI-FIGHTER WEAPON...

WHICH SECRET WEAPON?

THE APPLETREES!

HA HA HA HA HA HA

ON TUESDAY, JULY 18TH, THE AMERICAN TROOPS PENETRATE AS FAR AS ST.-LÔ...

PANG TAC TAC TAC TAC

INCREDIBLE! ALL THAT REMAINS HERE IS RUBBLE AND THEY'RE STILL SHOOTING!

YEP! THEY'RE FIGHTING FOR THE RUINS!

IT REMINDS ME OF THE GREAT WAR.

FOM JULY 18TH THROUGH 20 A GREAT ANGLO-CANADIAN OFFENSIVE, CALLED "GOODWOOD" IS LAUNCHED FROM THE EAST OF CAEN, PENETRATING SOUTHWARDS...

"TIGER" AT TWO O'CLOCK, SIR!

ANTI-TANK SHELL... RANGE...

BREACH STUCK, SIR!!!

SWOOP DOWN ON HIM! HIS GUN TURRET HASN'T PIVOTED YET!

DONNERWETTER!

GOTCHA!

VROOAW

BANG

LITTLE GROUND IS GAINED, BUT THE GERMANS ARE INCREASINGLY WEAKENED BY THE RELENTLESS COMBAT...

62

IN THEIR CAPACITY AS MEMBERS OF THE RESISTANCE, ADRIEN AND GASTON CAN APPROACH THE MILITARY INSTALLATIONS ON THE COAST...

IS IT SOLID, YOUR PORT?

YEAH! PROVIDED THAT THE ARTIFICIAL DYKE DESIGNED AS A BREAKWATER CAN WITHSTAND THE FORCE OF THE TIDE!

DO YOU REALISE THEY'VE BROUGHT AN ARTIFICIAL PORT WITH THEM!

UNBELIEVABLE!

HOW HAS THIS DYKE BEEN MADE?

...OLD SHIPS HAVE BEEN BALLASTED WITH CONCRETE AND SUNK ON THE SEABED.

... WE THEN REINFORCED THE BREAKWATER WITH ENORMOUS CONCRETE CUBES FILLED WITH WATER.

WOULD YOU CARE FOR A COCA-COLA, MONSIEUR ADRIEN? IT'S A TYPICALLY AMERICAN DRINK!

WHY NOT?

THE PORT WAS DESIGNED TO RECEIVE 7.000 TONS OF MERCHANDISE AND 1.250 VEHICLES EVERY DAY.

HOW CAN YOU DRINK THAT?

A STORM ON JUNE 19TH TO 20TH IS TO DAMAGE THE ARTIFICIAL PORTS AT OMAHA AND ARROMANCHES... ONLY THE LATTER IS WORTHY OF REPAIR.

THE ARROMANCHES MUSEUM

AT LOW TIDE TRACES OF THE ARTIFICIAL PORT OF ARROMANCHES CAN STILL BE SEEN. THE MUSEUM DISPLAYS A MAGNIFICENT MODEL OF THIS CONSTRUCTION, MEASURING ALMOST 20M IN LENGTH.

ON TUESDAY, JULY 25TH, 1.500 "FLYING FORTRESSES" APPEAR AMIDST THE CLOUDY SKIES TO THE WEST OF ST.-LÔ.

63

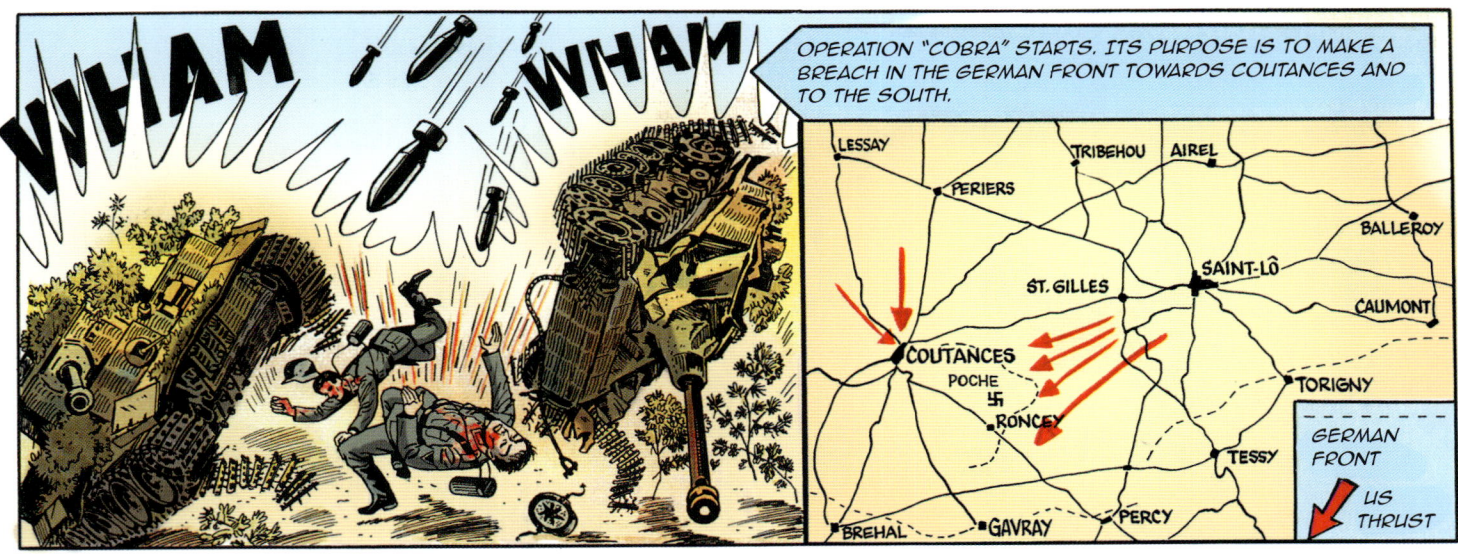

WHAM WHAM

OPERATION "COBRA" STARTS. ITS PURPOSE IS TO MAKE A BREACH IN THE GERMAN FRONT TOWARDS COUTANCES AND TO THE SOUTH.

THE BREAKTHROUGH SUCCEEDS AND ON JULY 28TH, THE US TANKS ARE AT THE GATES OF COUTANCES...

DON'T CRY, ARLETTE! WE'VE LEFT THE COMBAT ZONE! FOR US THE WAR IS OVER!

AT THE 11TH GERMAN PARACHUTE CORPS' HQ, NEAR PERCY...

I'M LT-COLONEL VON KLUGE, THE FELDMARSCHALL'S SON, GENERAL.

WHAT ARE YOU DOING HERE?

MY FATHER... ER... THE FELDMARSCHALL WANTS YOU TO HOLD OUT AND ASKS THAT THE TANKS...

WHICH TANKS?

THE PANZER LEHR DOESN'T EXIST ANYMORE AND THE FIGHTERS ARE GOING TO TRANSFORM OUR REMAINING UNITS INTO SMOKING WRECKS COLONEL!

ALL OF THESE ORDERS COME FROM PEOPLE WHO HAVEN'T THE FOGGIEST IDEA OF THE SITUATION!

FURTHERMORE, WE WERE EXPECTING AN EASTWARD AND SOUTH-EASTWARD ATTACK, BUT THAT DEVIL PATTON IS PUSHING SOUTH-WESTWARDS, FROM THE OTHER SIDE.

HE'LL BE IN AVRANCHES BY THE END OF THE MONTH!

INDEED, ON MONDAY, JULY 31ST, AVRANCHES IS TAKEN AND THE ADVANCE CONTINUES, PATTON IS RESTLESS...

HAVE A BULLDOZER CLEAN THIS UP! NOTHING MUST DELAY OUR PROGRESSION!

ON TUESDAY, AUGUST 1ST, IN THE UTAH AREA...

TAKE A BREATHER, BOYS! WE'RE HOME! IN FRANCE!

IN THE MUSEUM IN SAINTE-MÈRE-ÉGLISE

WORTH A DETOUR... AN IMPRESSIVE AMOUNT OF SOUVENIRS ARE GATHERED THERE. ESPECIALLY THIS EXAMPLE OF A DUMMY-PARACHUTIST THAT THE AMERICANS DROPPED ON CERTAIN REGIONS TO FOIL THE GERMANS...

THE 2ND FRENCH ARMOURED DIVISION JOINS PATTON 3RD ARMY...

ACTION! THE PERSON WITH THE BERET IS GENERAL LECLERC... THE OTHER ONE, WALKER.

UNDER THE COMMAND OF GENERAL LECLERC, THE 2ND DB HEADS STRAIGHT FOR THE FRONT AND, A FEW DAYS LATER, THE BELGIAN BRIGADE LANDS IN ARROMANCHES...

COLONEL PIRON.

UNDER THE ORDERS OF COLONEL PIRON THE BRIGADE IS PLACED UNDER THE COMMAND OF GENERAL GALE TO THE EAST OF THE ORNE...

I'M GLAD I CAME BY BOAT AND NOT ABOARD THOSE PLANES!

YEP! IT'S BADLY BRUISED!

ON SUNDAY, AUGUST 6TH, IN ST-GERMAIN-EN-LAYE...

FELDMARSCHALL VON KLUGE CALLING... GIVE ME THE FÜHRER... OH IT'S YOU, JODL... ACCORDING TO THE O.K.W.'S ORDERS...

I'VE MANAGED TO GATHER 400 TANKS AND 300 AIRPLANES. I WILL ATTACK TOMORROW!

NOT AT ALL, HERR MARSCHALL! YOU WILL ONLY START THE COUNTER OFFENSIVE ON AUGUST 8TH!

VILLEDIEU ST SEVER • CONDÉ
• BRÉCEY FLERS
AVRANCHES
MORTAIN

FOUGERES

IF I WAIT ONE MORE DAY, THE FIGHTERS ARE GOING TO SPOT MY TANKS!

THESE ARE THE FÜHRER'S ORDERS!

THE O.K.W. WAS LOOKING TO SLOW DOWN THE GERMAN BREAKTHROUGH TO ENSNARE A MAXIMUM NUMBER OF ENEMY TROOPS...

NEIN! I WILL ATTACK TOMORROW REGARDLESS!

AT THE SAME TIME, IN THE CITY...

THE GERMAN "GREY MICE" ARE TAKING TO THEIR HEELS... THAT'S A GOOD SIGN!

YES, AND THE "FRITZ"(1) HAVE REQUISITIONED ALL THE BICYCLES!

(1) GERMANS

THE NEXT DAY, AT DAYBREAK...

I CAN'T SEE ANYTHING IN THIS FOG!

DON'T MOAN, THE JABOS ARE SURE TO LEAVE US IN PEACE!

OUR PLANES WILL TAKE CARE OF THEM!

THE OFFENSIVE TOWARDS THE WEST (MORTAIN, AVRANCHES AND THE SEA) IS INTENDED TO CUT OFF AMERICAN SUPPLIES, BUT BY NOON...

THE GERMAN AIRPLANES HAD ALL BEEN PINNED TO THE GROUND OR DESTROYED AT TAKE-OFF...

WHAM

THE GERMAN COUNTER-ATTACK FAILS AND THE FÜHRER FAILS TO CONTAIN HIS RAGE...

VON KLUGE HAS DELIBERATELY MADE THE OPERATION A FAILURE! MY ORDERS WERE CLEAR ENOUGH!

66

IN ST. GERMAIN-EN-LAYE...

IT'S A BAD DAY, MEN!

YOU BET! THE AMERICAN PLANES ARE MACHINE-GUNNING ALL OUR TRAINS...

THEY SAY THAT PATTON'S TANKS ARE PUSHING INTO BRITTANY, THAT DOESN'T HELP EITHER!

EVEN IF PATTON'S ADVANCE IS DEVASTATING, THE GERMAN FRONT IS RESISTING WELL TO THE SOUTH OF CAUMONT AND VILLERS-BOCAGE. MEANWHILE SGT RILEY IN HIS TANK...

IT'S TOO CALM... SOMETHING'S BREWING!

ACHTUNG! A SHERMAN!

WOUFF

BAM

FEUER!

HURRY UP! EVERYTHING'S GOING TO EXPLODE! QUICK!

THE REST OF MY CREW IS TRAPPED IN THE TANK!

IN THE HOUSE ON THE OTHER SIDE OF THE STREET...

DOES HE MEAN THAT THE KRAUTS ARE UPSTAIRS?

THROW A GRENADE... I'LL GO UPSTAIRS...

67

A LITTLE LATER...

THIS IS EXACTLY WHAT I PREDICTED: THE AMERICAN GUNS HAVE FLATTENED CINTHEAUX[1]

(1) VILLAGE ON THE CAEN-FALAISE ROAD...

WE'RE GOING TO SETTLE THERE... WITTMANN'S "TIGERS" WILL COVER OUR FLANKS... GO AND WARN HIM, KERNER!

VROOO

THE 28TH CANADIAN REGIMENT'S ATTACKS ENCOUNTER THE DEFENSIVE LINE INSTALLED BY "PANZER-MEYER"

BAM TAC TAC TAC

MICHAËL WITTMANN IS LOOKING TO GATHER MORE TANKS AS HUNTING TROPHIES...

THAT'S FOR ME!

FORWARD!

BUT THERE ARE FIVE OF THEM!

SURPRISE IS OUR ADVANTAGE! FULL THROTTLE!

WITTMANN MEETS WITH DEATH AT DUSK ON AUGUST 8TH, AMIDST THE SKIRMISH...

HIS BODY WAS ONLY TO BE RECOVERED IN MAY 1983.

71

A LITTLE FURTHER EASTWARDS, ALTHOUGH WITH THE "HITLERJUGEND" HOT ON THEIR TRAIL, THE 1ST POLISH TANK DIVISION. (LANDED AT THE END OF JULY) MOVES TOWARDS FALAISE... IT IS UNDER THE COMMAND OF GENERAL MACZEK...

LOOK AT THE MAP... WITH THE CANADIANS WE ARE A DOZEN KILOMETRES AWAY FROM FALAISE...

IF PATTON'S TANK PROCEED AT THE PRESENT PACE, THEY'LL TAKE ARGENTAN IN LESS THAN A WEEK...

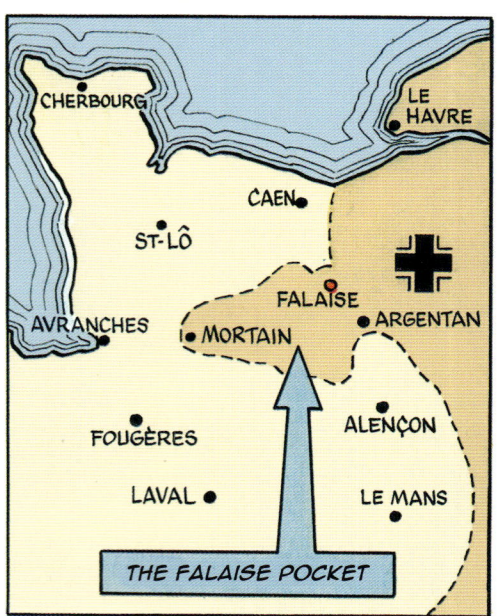

THE FALAISE POCKET

CHERBOURG
LE HAVRE
CAEN
ST-LÔ
AVRANCHES
FALAISE
MORTAIN
ARGENTAN
FOUGÈRES
ALENÇON
LAVAL
LE MANS

THERE ARE TWENTY ODD KILOMETRES BETWEEN FALAISE AND ARGENTAN... WE CAN ENCLOSE THE 7TH GERMAN ARMY COMPLETELY AND DESTROY IT!

SEVERAL ALLIED GENERALS (AND MORE PARTICULARLY PATTON AND LECLERC) HAVE THE SAME IDEA... ON SATURDAY, AUGUST 12TH, THE FRENCH 2ÈME D.B. ENTERS ALENÇON...

IF WE CONTINUE OUR ADVANCE AT THIS SPEED, WE'LL CLOSE THE DOOR FOR THE GERMANS...

NEAR FALAISE...

HEY, LOOK DOWN, DAN... IF THEY DON'T HURRY TO CLOSE "THE POCKET", THEY WON'T FIND ANYONE THERE ANYMORE!

I DON'T UNDERSTAND WHY THE COMMAND IS SLOWING PATTON'S PROGRESS DOWN!

IN CREULLY CASTLE (NOT FAR FROM MONTGOMERY'S HQ)...

THIS IS THE BBC, CHESTER WILMOT ON THE AIR. TODAY, AUGUST 15TH, AFTER AIR AND NAVAL BOMBINGS, THE FRANCO-AMERICAN FORCES LANDED IN THE SOUTH OF FRANCE, IN PROVENCE...

WHEREAS IN THE CASTLE AT LA ROCHE-GUYON...

WHAT'S HAPPENING?

WHERE ARE YOU GOING WITH THAT?

TO HIDE THESE OBJECTS, YOU NEVER KNOW WITH THE LATEST EVENTS...

IN ST.-GERMAIN-EN-LAYE...

YOU MUST GO TO BEAUVAIS "BY YOUR OWN MEANS"? IS THAT A JOKE?

NO, THE SIMPLE IDEA OF SUCH A LONG MARCH, NO DANGER!

... I'VE STOLEN THE AIDE-DE-CAMP'S BIKE... IN REVENGE FOR ALL THE TIMES HE YELLED AT ME!

THE NEWS OF THE LANDING IN PROVENCE, ALONG WITH THE PREDICTABLE COLLAPSE OF THE FRONT OF NORMANDY, UNLEASHES MURDEROUS MADNESS IN SOME GERMAN UNITS.

SUMMARY EXECUTIONS OF RESISTANCE FIGHTERS, HOSTAGES AND SUSPECTS ARE RIFE...

THESE OUTRAGES PROVOKE BLIND RETALIATION...

A FRITZ!

SOLDIER DOLF SCHÖRNER LEAVES ST.-GERMAIN-EN-LAYE...

AFTER THE WAR, I'LL COME BACK HERE... AS A TOURIST...

71

PANG!

ON AUGUST 16TH, COMMANDO 4 IS ORDERED TO ATTACK...

APPARENTLY WE'RE PREPARING A HUGE OFFENSIVE TO CRUSH THE KRAUTS...

THAT'S WHAT THEY'VE BEEN TELLING US SINCE D-DAY!

PANG!

LE SAULT IS HURT...

AAAH!

FLUSH OUT THAT SNIPER!

ICH ERGEBE MICH(1)

SALAUD!

(1) I SURRENDER

I DON'T SURRENDER TO FRENCHMEN!

YOU DON'T EH!

BOF

LEAVE HIM ALONE! HE'LL PULL THROUGH! EVACUATE HIM!

MEANWHILE, IN GERMANY...

YES, IT'S ME MANFRED ROMMEL, COLONEL!

YOUR FATHER HAS LEFT THE FRENCH HOSPITAL...HE HAS RETURNED HOME... YOU HAVE A LEAVE PASS.

LATER IN THE FELDMARCHALL'S HOUSE...

THEY'VE BEEN LOOKING TO ELIMINATE ME SINCE THE FAILED ATTEMPT ON THE FÜHRER...

BUT...

NO QUESTIONS MANFRED! KEEP THIS WITH YOU AND TAKE CARE OF YOUR MOTHER!

UPON HITLER'S ORDERS, THE GESTAPO FORCE ROMMEL TO COMMIT SUICIDE IN OCTOBER 1944.

(1) ON JULY 20TH, 1944

ON FRIDAY, AUGUST 18TH, IN LA ROCHE-GUYON, JUST BEFORE DAYBREAK...

AT A TIME WHEN LA ROCHE-GUYON IS ALREADY UNDER AMERICAN GUNFIRE, I BID YOU FAREWELL... AS YOU KNOW, THE FÜHRER DISMISSED ME FROM COMMAND YESTERDAY...

I HAVE UNDERTAKEN TO DIRECT THE 7TH ARMY'S WITHDRAWAL BEHIND THE RIVER SEINE BUT I'M AFRAID IT'S ALREADY TOO LATE! GOOD LUCK, GENTLEMEN!

MARSCHALL VON KLUGE POISONED HIMSELF THE SAME DAY.

BETWEEN AUGUST 18TH AND 20TH, THE "FALAISE POCKET" CLOSES ONCE MORE... THE 120.000 MEN WHO RUN FROM THE ENCIRCLEMENT. FIRST IN AN ORDERLY MANNER, THEN IN EXTREME CONFUSION BECAUSE OF THE BOMBINGS...

IF YOU GET OUT, WRITE TO MY HOME!

YES, I DO!

OK! YOU KNOW WE'VE ONLY GOT AN 8KM-WIDE CORRIDOR TO ESCAPE FROM THE CARNAGE?

ON SUNDAY, AUGUST 20TH, WITH THE REMAINS OF THE 12TH PANZER SS, NORTHEAST OF FALAISE, "PANZER"-MEYER...

GENTLEMEN! I HAVE THE ORDER TO WITHDRAW OUR DIVISION TO THE REAR OF THE FRONT LINE WE'LL TRY TO CROSS THE RIVER DIVES IN SAINT-LAMBERT, AT NOON SHARP!

YOUR "DIVISION"... YOU MEAN YOUR BRATS TRANSFORMED INTO KILLING MACHINES! IT'S RIDICULOUS!

THE JOKE'S ON YOU! YOU LOOK LIKE A CLOWN WITH YOUR GIRL'S BIKE!

CLOWN? YOU'LL SEE...

HERE OUR TANKS ARE RUNNING OVER CORPSES TO ESCAPE FROM THIS HELL... NOT ONLY WILL YOU BE DEAD BUT YOU'LL TOTALLY DISAPPEAR!

THAT'LL DO, KERNER! ... AND YOU, GET OUT OF HERE! GET READY, GENTLEMEN!

IN SAINT-LAMBERT, WHERE THE CANADIANS ARE IN CONTROL OF THE BRIDGES OVER THE DIVES...

MAIS...

GIVE A SIGNAL TO "PANZER"-MEYER!

TAC TAC TAC TAC

BAM

TAC TAC TAC TAC

THE 2ND PANZER, THE 10TH PANZER SS, THE 116TH PANZER AND OTHER UNITS RUSH TOWARDS THE BRIDGE OVER THE DIVES, TO CLEAR THE WAY, VEHICLES, HORSES AND THE WOUNDED ARE DUMPED INTO THE RAVINE...

ON AUGUST 20TH, THE "POCKET" IS CLOSED, THE ARTILLERY AND THE AIR FORCE BLUDGEON THE ENSNARED TROOPS...

LOOK AT THAT, DAN... KILOMETRES OF CORPSES AND BURNING WRECKS!

M. Kit.

I HOPE THE WORLD WILL NEVER SEE SUCH HORROR AGAIN!

VROAWWW

FILL UP THE MOTORCYCLE!

THERE'S NO MORE FUEL, HERR USTUF...

FIND SOME!

WHERE ARE YOU GOING, KERNER?

I'M LEAVING YOU, HERR BRIGADEFÜHRER! WE'VE LOST THE WAR!

YOU'RE CRAZY!

NO, HERR BRIGADEFÜHRER... BETWEEN THE DEAD, THE WOUNDED AND THE PRISONERS, IN ALL WE'VE LOST HALF A MILLION MEN... WE SIMPLY CAN'T RECOVER!

VROM VROM

75

THE WAR WILL SOON BE AT AN END. AND THERE'S NOTHING I CAN DO. WHAT WILL BECOME OF ME?

I'LL JUST CONTINUE TO DO THE ONLY THING I'VE EVER LEARNED... FAREWELL, BRIGADEFÜHRER!

KERNER!

VROOP

VRAOWW

A LITTLE FURTHER ON, NEAR THE POSITIONS HELD BY THE CANADIANS, NORTHEAST OF SAINT-LAMBERT...

!!!

VROOOAW

IT'S HIM!

IT'S THAT SS!

HE'S RIDING STRAIGHT INTO THE ZONE THE ARTILLERY IS WIPING OUT!

VROAA AWL

WHAM

WOUFF

76

THE "BATTLE OF FALAISE" ENDS ON TUESDAY MORNING, AUGUST 22ND, AND THE SAME DAY...

TO ALL UNITS... WE HAVE FINALLY RECEIVED ORDERS TO HEAD FOR PARIS...

THE 2ÈME D.B. ADVANCES ON TO RAMBOUILLET...

SEND A MESSAGE TO THE PARISIANS WHO HAVE TAKEN UP ARMS AGAINST THE ENEMY: WE'RE ON OUR WAY! DON'T GIVE UP!

THE BELGIAN BRIGADE HAS LIBERTATED CABOURG, DEAUVILLE, HONFLEUR... AND IS PREPARING TO ATTACK LE HAVRE...

HONFLEUR

COMMANDO 4 TAKES PONT L'ÉVÊQUE WHICH THE GERMANS HAVE SET ON FIRE...

THERE ARE ENGLISH PRISONERS IN THE BURNING FELDKOMMANDANTUR! IT'S NEARBY!

YOU'VE ARRIVED JUST IN TIME, BOYS!

KOMMANDATUR

WHERE ARE YOU FROM?

FROM OUISTREHAM! WE'VE BEEN FIGHTING ENDLESSLY FOR TEN WEEKS NOW AND WITH ALMOST NO SLEEP...

ONLY 177 FRENCHMEN LANDED... BUT WE DESERVED TO BE HERE!

MEANWHILE, ON THE BANKS OF THE SEINE, SOUTH OF ROUEN...

YOUR NAME? MEN AND VEHICLES?..

BRIGADEFÜHRER KURT MEYER, 12TH PANZER SS... 280 MEN SAVED AND 18 VEHICLES INCLUDING 10 TANKS.

THANKS TO FLOATING BRIDGES (DISASSEMBLED AND HIDDEN DURING THE DAY) THE TROOPS HAVING ESCAPED FROM THE FALAISE POCKET CONTINUE THEIR WITHDRAWAL.

IS THAT ALL?

SADLY!

THEN YOU CAN LEAVE, HERR BRIGADEFÜHRER... GOOD LUCK!

GOOD LUCK, TO YOU TOO!

THE NEXT DAY AT BASE B7

WHERE'S YOUR BOSS? I WANT TO HAVE A WORD WITH HIM, I'M FED UP WITH YOUR STUNTS...

... THEY FRIGHTEN MY COWS AND IT'S NO GOOD FOR THEIR MILK!

VRROOOO

BUT GIVE THIS BOTTLE TO YOUR MEN... WITH ALL MY PRAISE, BECAUSE I'VE HAD ENOUGH OF YOUR WAR...

OF "OUR" WAR?

RANGERS MUSEUM

ATTACK ON POINTE DU HOC

LT.-COLONEL J.E. RUDDER

LOCATED IN GRANDCAMP-MAISY. SOUVENIRS OF THE FAMOUS EPIC TALE OF THE RANGERS AWAIT YOUR VISIT.

MUCH LATER, WHEN THE "BATTLE OF NORMANDY" SEEMS BUT A DISTANT MEMORY...

OUR COMMAND FAILED TO WORK TO PERFECTION... IF ONLY WE HAD ACCELERATED IN CLOSING THE FALAISE POCKET...

... ONCE AND FOR ALL, WE WOULD HAVE ELIMINATED THE ELITE GERMAN TROOPS WE ENCOUNTERED LATER!

THAT'S TRUE MONTY⁽¹⁾... WE ALSO FAILED TO PREVENT THOSE UNITS FROM CROSSING THE SEINE...

(1) MONTGOMERY'S NICKNAME AMONG HIS FRIENDS.

BUT THE SAME UNITS HAVE LOST ALMOST ALL THEIR EQUIPMENT AND MORE PARTICULARLY THEY'VE LOST THEIR BEST SOLDIERS!

WE KNOW... THAT IS UNDENIABLE... ER... DO YOU REMEMBER, MONTY, THAT RAIN-BEATEN NIGHT IN JUNE WHEN WE SAID...

..."TUEDAY, JUNE 6ᵀᴴ WILL BE *D-DAY*". DID A SINGLE ONE OF US NOT FEAR DEFEAT?

THE END

SCRIPT: SERGE SAINT-MICHEL - DRAWINGS: MISTER KIT - COLOURS: MARTINE BOUTIN

82

Thanks to:

Mme I. BOURNIER
M. P. CAPRON
M. M. CHAUVET
M. R. DESQUESNES
M. N. DUMONT
M. J.-M. LEFRANC
M. J. LONGUET
The Lyme Regis Library

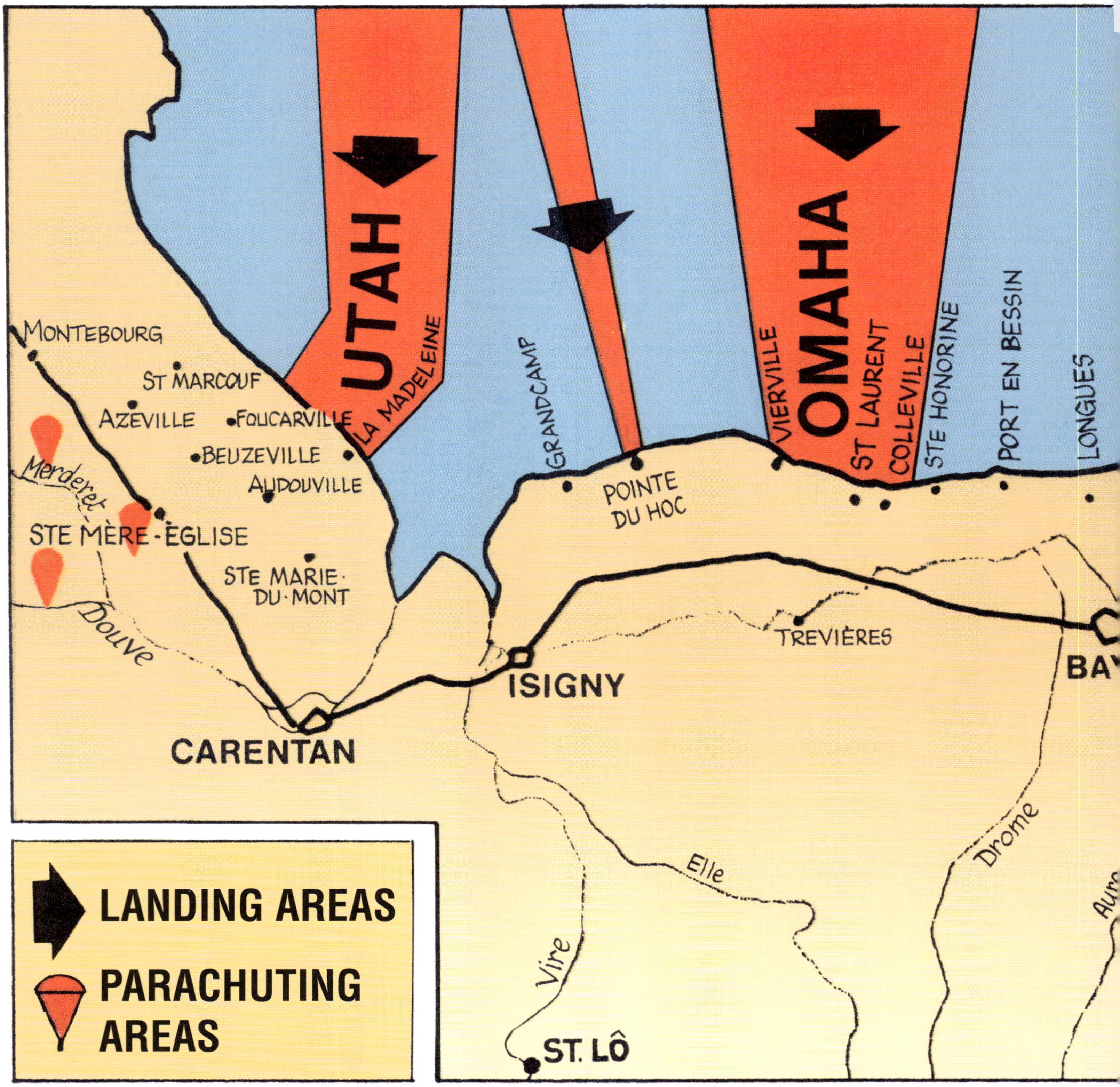

MONTEBOURG

ST MARCOUF

AZEVILLE • FOUCARVILLE

UTAH

LA MADELEINE

• BEUZEVILLE

AUDOUVILLE

Merderet

STE MÈRE-ÈGLISE

STE MARIE·
DU·MONT

Douve

CARENTAN

GRANDCAMP

POINTE
DU HOC

VIERVILLE

OMAHA

ST LAURENT

COLLEVILLE

STE HONORINE

PORT EN BESSIN

LONGUES

ISIGNY

TREVIÈRES

BAY

Elle

Drome

Aure

Vire

ST. LÔ

LANDING AREAS

PARACHUTING
AREAS